The AI Tsunami

A Survival Guide for Humanity

GUY MORRIS

SUNBURY PRESS
Mechanicsburg, PA USA

Published by Sunbury Press, Inc.
Mechanicsburg, PA USA

www.sunburypress.com

FIRST SUNBURY PRESS EDITION: July 2026

Set in Adobe Garamond | Interior design by Crystal Devine | Cover by Lawrence Knorr | Edited by Gabrielle Kirk.

Publisher's Cataloging-in-Publication Data
Names: Morris, Guy, author.
Title: The AI tsunami : a survival guide for humanity / Guy Morris.
Description: First trade paperback edition. | Mechanicsburg, PA : Sunbury Press, 2026.
Summary: Artificial intelligence is a rising tsunami reshaping every job, business, and culture. The AI Tsunami explains the promise, the dangers, and practical strategies to adapt, reskill, and thrive—so you can ride the wave instead of being swept away by it.
Identifiers: ISBN : 979-8-88819-460-7 (paperback).
Subjects: COMPUTERS / Artificial Intelligence / General | BUSINESS & ECONOMICS / Careers / General | POLITICAL SCIENCE / Public Policy / Science & Technology Policy | PHILOSOPHY / Ethics & Moral Philosophy.

Designed in the USA
0 1 1 2 3 5 8 13 21 34 55

For the Love of Books!

This book was a labor of love for my friends and readers who struggle to understand the full scope of the coming AI tsunami. I dedicate this book to the auburn Irish beauty who patiently endured all the stories, warnings, rants, tribulations, and the obsessive hours it took to bring this book to life. To Darcy, my angel.

CONTENTS

DISCLAIMER

Substantial research went into the development and writing of this book. However, because of rapidly changing technologies, as well as enterprise, government, and labor market changes, some of the information or URL links provided will be dated at some point.

However, the trends, principles, and overall analysis will remain valid. The reader may want to research the latest studies as they develop their personal or small business strategy.

NOTABLE QUOTES

"There are three inevitable events with AI. AI will happen. AI will be smarter than humans. Bad things will happen."

—Mo Gawdat

"With artificial intelligence, we are summoning the demon."

—Elon Musk

"I don't think it's inherent that as we create superintelligence that it will necessarily always have the same goals in mind as we do."

—Bill Gates

"The development of full artificial intelligence could spell the end of the human race . . . It would take off on its own and redesign itself at an ever-increasing rate. Humans, who are limited by slow biological evolution, couldn't compete and would be superseded."

—Stephen Hawking

"Our intelligence is what makes us human, and AI is an extension of that quality."

—Yann LeCun

"Nobody phrases it this way, but I think that artificial intelligence is almost a humanities discipline. It's really an attempt to understand human intelligence and human cognition."

—Sebastian Thrun

Foreword

I have been watching this wave build for thirty years.

Not as a bystander. As someone who was in the water when the early systems came online. Expert systems. Rules engines. Neural nets that ate hardware budgets and returned mostly disappointment. I watched the field cycle through its seasons of hype and silence. I learned to read the signs. So, when Guy Morris uses the word tsunami, I don't think he's being dramatic. I think he's being precise.

That matters. In a space full of breathless proclamations and existential panic, precision is rare. This book has it.

I spend a lot of time thinking about what happens when technology outpaces the human systems built around it. Not technology itself, because technology is never the hard part. The hard part is the people. The organizations. The habits and assumptions baked into how we work and live. Those don't change on a product release schedule.

What Guy has done here is unusual. He's written a book about technological transformation that keeps pulling the conversation back to people. Back to the human equation. I find that refreshing. Most books about AI get lost in machinery. This one keeps asking the harder question: What does this mean for us?

I've seen migrations go badly. I've seen organizations treat change management as an afterthought, then spend years cleaning up the wreckage. Thirty years of enterprise consulting leaves you with a certain clarity about what matters when the ground shifts. It's not technology. It's whether the people who depend on it have what they need to adapt.

That's the purpose of being a survival guide. Not to frighten. To prepare.

Guy walks you through history, the risk, the opportunity, and the strategy. He doesn't pretend the outcome is settled. It's not. Nobody knows exactly what the shoreline looks like on the other side of this wave. Anyone who tells you otherwise is selling something. What we do know and what this book makes clear is that the people who understand what's coming and take deliberate steps will be far better than those who don't.

I am rarely surprised by where technology lands. But I am always surprised by how long it takes people to realize it has landed. That gap between reality and awareness is where most of the damage happens. This book narrows the gap. That's a valuable thing.

Read it with an open mind. Take the warnings seriously. Take the opportunities seriously, too. The future Guy is describing isn't a binary utopia or catastrophe. It's messier than that, and more interesting. And the choices you make in the next few years will matter more than you probably expect.

The wave is already in motion. Time to find higher ground. Make sure you keep your copy of *The AI Tsunami Survival Guide* dry; you will need it after the wave hits.

Scott Andersen
Author, *Infrastructure for AI Network Design and Architecture*

CHAPTER 1

A Tsunami is Coming!

Look up! A tsunami is coming! Quick, find higher ground!

Powerful, destructive, and transformative waves of change will reach the shores of every nation, every culture, nearly every job role, and nearly every aspect of our modern, connected world.

An artificial intelligence tsunami that few are prepared to face will reshape the shoreline of society for decades and centuries to come. While tech leaders and their champions praise this revolution, they obscure the fact that only a few will benefit immensely as hundreds of millions of people are displaced or subjugated by greater business and government control.

A tsunami is an unstoppable force of nature, generating waves that seem distant in time and place until they wreak havoc and destruction. Waves of change that will rewrite the course of human history to usher in a time of technological advancement beyond anything ever witnessed.

The Iron and Bronze Ages, the printing press, electricity, the telephone, and computers are among the amazing advancements in human history. Each of these empowered a human to do more, faster and cheaper than before. Never in history have we created something that could exceed our capabilities and act on its own, a machine smarter than any human on the planet with the ability to improve itself on its own will. Until this point, our inventions enhanced the capabilities of humans. We have reached a fundamental paradigm shift where we are building machines to replace humans and make decisions that will affect the lives of real people.

In 1942, Austrian economist Joseph Schumpeter introduced the concept of Creative Destruction, which describes how new technologies or innovations can create wealth and structure at the expense of destroying the old wealth and structures. Artificial Intelligence and related technologies may be the most powerful destruction and creation in human history.

While we are helpless against the force when it lands, we can read the signs to prepare before the waves build up. Now is the time to prepare.

I wish it were only hyperbole. It's not. There is a profound and conflicted truth in the future we share. A future that will hold seemingly miraculous achievements, alongside the devastation of careers, privacy, social norms, justice, and our democratic freedoms.

Powering this tsunami will be the long-sought emergence of commercial, government, and military-grade machine intelligence. No longer the stuff of science fiction, but a powerful, transformative technology that has already seen adoption rates skyrocket. Over a trillion dollars of investment and growing promises a fresh wave of technology-driven miracles in healthcare, science, education, and creativity. These technologies also bring a terrifying and imminent threat to our way of life.

Knowledge is Power

The goal of this book is to empower the reader with a deeper knowledge of this emerging technology, the astounding potential, and the undeniable risks it will bring. To thrive during these coming waves of change, the reader will need both a knowledge of the opportunities and success strategies, as well as the dangers and pitfalls to avoid.

For individuals facing a future of uncertain employment, this book will prepare them with broad knowledge, choices, and an entire chapter dedicated to building a 90-day strategic roadmap.

For small or medium businesses that seek to gain a competitive edge, lower costs, and empower their workforce, this book will provide a high-level and thoughtful approach to navigating the transition to an intelligence-enabled workforce to minimize costs and optimize performance.

For concerned citizens and policymakers worried about the legislative, regulatory, social, and political impacts of machine intelligence, *The AI Tsunami Survival Guide* will illuminate the legal, financial, moral, and social implications.

Most of all, we must keep redirecting the conversation away from technology to focus on the human side of the equation. How will machine intelligence technology and the emerging AI economy affect our lives, shared society, safety, privacy, the business environment, banking, government, and the world as we know it?

Not interested in writing a technical treatise for nerds, the goal of this book was to write a survival guide for our humanity.

Big Bang

Artificial intelligence exploded in the public awareness in November 2022 when a little-known open-source research company called OpenAI released a free product called ChatGPT to the world. Within three months, over one hundred million people had signed up, faster than any software service in history, forcing competitors to rethink their market strategies. Several companies released their AI products to the market, some pre-maturely. It motivated investors to commit hundreds of billions to the dream of an intelligent machine future. By 2025, over four hundred separate products, platforms, technologies, or AI-upgrades to existing products had hit the market.

Rarely does a single product launch raise the level of both excitement and unbridled panic in so short a time. People who know absolutely nothing about AI either hate it, won't touch it, or see the new tech as the savior of humanity. All are overreactions.

Nearly every major tech company works on an AI platform. A platform is the technical foundation on which to build other intelligent applications. IBM, Apple, Google, Microsoft, Oracle, OpenAI, Anthropic, and dozens of other startups and partnerships have formed. By 2026, new investments in AI tech exploded to over a trillion dollars once new private power sources to support massive neural networks are factored into the equation. And the investment is still rising. With a market capitalization in the multiple trillions, a dot-com boom on Android steroids with unpredictable outcomes.

When we factor in other related technologies such as quantum computing, neuromorphic computing, cryptology, high-performance chips, and other related sciences, we are at the threshold of a technological renaissance unlike any seen in history, even surpassing the computer revolution itself.

A pivot point in the evolution of civilization. A change so broad and profound as to reflect a paradigm shift for humanity with almost zero serious public dialogue about whether we should.

We've heard a wide variety of predictions—ranging from *Terminator* to an Apple version of Rosie the Robot in every home. Dreams of a technical utopia clash hard with equally dystopic nightmares of a Borg robotic takeover led by Zuckerberg, Musk, Nadella, Ellison, and Altman, each demanding we assimilate.

Many experts envision a path to a *Star Trek*-style utopia where everyone has a great education and meaningful jobs. Perhaps through a process of both technical and social innovation, we will resolve traditional human problems such as poverty, food security, petty crime, sickness, or other inherited disorders, and even addiction or mental illness. Medical techniques such as surgery will be outdated, replaced by surgical robots. World governments will unite around universal healthcare, a universal basic income, and instantaneous fact-checking of leadership to hold them accountable to the truth. Innovations in science, materials, and physics could expand the scope of our existence to Mars and beyond. Interactive creative tools can transform even those with no talent into joyful creators, and elevate gifted creators to new, unimagined heights. The potential of machine intelligence is almost unlimited.

The reality will be nothing like any of the predictions, but maybe a little like all of them.

What I can say with absolute certainty is that unless you live off the grid or in a remote emerging economy or an island, machine intelligence will touch your life. It already has in ways you don't see. Some of the changes have been invisible, hidden behind how the world operates, or hidden in plain sight in the mobile device you carry.

Brilliant minds will find solutions and create innovations faster, cheaper, and with better integration of computing technology to humans using machine speech. For those craving a prosperous and next-generation direction for their business, art, or career, AI is the next gold rush dream for investors. Survival is the foundation on which to thrive. We'll talk a little about both.

As such, many fresh developments will seem opaque and harmless. Other changes will be stark, abrupt, and so disruptive that they will demand a national, business, and individual response. We'll get to those later.

We no longer have a choice. The ship has sailed. The train has left the station. Massacre all the metaphors you want, but the AI tsunami is already unstoppable. Neural network powered intelligence will become smarter than humans, and both good and bad things are bound to occur.

Yet we are not powerless, nor without a voice or a choice. Those choices are the reason this book was written. *The AI Tsunami Survival Guide* will look at all perspectives. The good and the bad, the exciting and the scary, the risks and opportunities. Elephants in the room, beware.

A Human Story

The truth is simple. The coming tsunami is not about the technology. It's about our shared humanity, our communities, families, and personal futures.

The AI tsunami is about the changes to our way of life, job security, plans, strategies to adapt, loss of privacy, mental health, basic needs, spirituality, national security, social contract, and more. We face a paradigm shift in human development with potentially dark consequences.

Sometimes in history, a single technology can pivot the direction of civilization, for better or worse. Fire, written language, the printing press, gunpowder, electricity, computers, the internet, cell phones, and others all brought good and bad outcomes. None of these revolutionary changes were able to operate on their own, improve on their own, speak on their own, act on their own, or have the capacity to be smarter than any human on the planet. They were tools, not competition. That paradigm has changed.

We are not looking at a temporary historical blip or glitch. The AI tsunami will bring about a fundamental change in our civilization for you, me, our children, and grandchildren for generations to come. A disruptive change to how the world works, how societies will function, where we work, how we get our basic needs met, and how those with power will exercise that power to keep us under control. Some of the changes will be gradual and subtle, while other changes will be an unwelcome surprise.

The AI tsunami is also a story of opportunity, new horizons, new chances to solve intractable world problems, and create new breakthroughs in science, medicine, education, and human relationships. Astounding accomplishments that were never possible before now. Like nuclear energy, we face an incredible paradox of good and evil represented in one technology. The choices we make now will either benefit or curse our society for generations to come.

Machine intelligence will create entirely new alternative career paths and enhance education and training opportunities around the world. Intelligent assistants will do the mundane tasks so we can focus on what matters most. Machines will help develop innovative solutions to climate change, new drugs, new cures, and new materials for space travel. Imagine unbiased decision-makers throughout our society, removing corruption, ignorance and neglect.

Small businesses will gain a competitive edge, empowering employees to do exponentially more with less effort, interjecting insights and best practices into the business. Product innovations will come to market in record time with improved customer support and service. Implementing AI will not be a simple business choice, but a competitive imperative.

Machine intelligence will change the world in profound, dynamic, and life-altering ways.

But there's a catch. There will be clear winners and losers in this transformation. There will be people prepared and others left behind. The wealth-gap crisis will grow exponentially to transform our society into a techno-autocratic feudalism.

Unless we raise our voices in unity. Unless we make the right choice for our personal security.

Hope and Choice

Welcome to the first quiet moments of the AI tsunami, when the world seems normal, and yet we sense something is wrong. We witness the ocean pulling back from the shore. A warning of what is coming.

The AI Tsunami Survival Guide will provide a clear, but simplified and non-technical understanding of this astounding technology, which has been seven decades in the making. You will learn a little AI history, about the various forms of AI, stages of AI, key uses you already see today, key risks you don't see, and the next stages of development coming soon.

Most importantly, this book will focus on choices. Careers. Families. Relationships. Homes. Education. Security. Privacy. Freedom. Culture. Politics. Justice. I want to empower the reader to make better choices for themselves and family in the face of these changes.

After reading this book, you will be better prepared for what will be a new golden era for some, and turbulent or desperate times for others. And likely a mix of both for the rest of us.

Humanity is not helpless. You are not helpless or without options. Part of the trick to surviving a tsunami is a rapid response. Delays can be deadly. The world is changing fast, and we all need to find higher ground. A tsunami is coming, but don't worry. You have an *AI Tsunami Survival Guide*.

CHAPTER 2

Flashback: A Personal Journey

When I speak of the humanity of this technology, part of that story is personal. You see, AI and I were born in the same month at different ends of the country. In a strange way, the story of AI and my personal story align, connecting key professional milestones. Perhaps I should start with a quick self-introduction and a brief explanation of why I wrote this book.

Change My Stars

After attending sixteen different schools before leaving home functionally illiterate at age fifteen, and desperate to change my stars, I stumbled onto a chance to attend a state university. A miracle, really, and widely seen as a personal long shot at best. Yet, I graduated with a bachelor's degree in both economics and finance with a minor in computer science from the University of Arizona. Landing on the Dean's List with a full grad school scholarship, an internship at IBM, I was also accepted into the Harvard MBA program. The Federal Reserve even sent me a friendly letter of congratulations.

To win that scholarship, I bet with the college dean that I could design a macroeconomic model (graduation assignment) that would outperform every student in the school based on an unproven theory I had developed. That model outperformed the Federal Reserve and changed how the world builds economic models to this day. I had developed and integrated the first algorithm to predict the value of technology-driven productivity on GDP. An old-school nerd-zilla was born.

It's important to note this 1970s era geeky achievement because macroeconomic modeling uses many of the same techniques, algorithms, nonlinear, and other advanced regression mathematics as modern artificial intelligence. Both require vast amounts of data and complex layers of interconnected algorithms or complex formulas. Only before the age of big data, cloud storage, neuro-networks, and machine learning, nerds like me had to design and build the data model, construct the sub-models, and write the regression algorithms manually.

Instead of using machine learning to perform millions of simulations to tweak the hundreds of parameters, nerds like me would sit in a data center basement, connected by terminal to an IBM mainframe to run endless simulations.

Yes, it was as painful as it sounds. Let's move on before my left eye starts to twitch again.

Expert Systems

Fast forward a few years when I implemented an experimental platform called Expert Systems. At the time, I worked for a major international oil and gas exploration company that also operated major petrochemical plants, coal mines, other diverse subsidiaries, with a trading office in Moscow. Responsible for managing operational audit teams on every continent, we wrote our reports for the board of directors. You can imagine the pressure for perfection.

The idea was to train the system to mimic the operational analysis, decision process, key factors, and recommended actions of a subject-matter expert. Our goal was to empower the more junior (and cheaper) resources on a remote operational audit, without the risks and costs of also sending an expensive expert three thousand miles into jungles infested with drug cartels and militia. Great in concept, not so much in execution.

Like many new technologies, there were pros and cons. These systems demanded an enormous amount of data necessary to work effectively, as well as a significant amount of time from a subject-matter expert to map potential scenarios, and more effort to encode it into the system. The system operated using brute-force training by a business user. Me, or someone on my team, mostly. Not uncommon for complex software of the time, but it was a big negative in my view.

Because we were early adopters of an experimental tech on an international scale, we met with designers from IBM and DARPA (Defense Advanced Research Projects Administration) to debrief on project issues. We needed *way* more industry-wide data. And *way* more power to analyze that data for the scenarios we didn't expect.

The industry had work to do. But out of that phase came some key insights about intelligence. Within five years, all areas we addressed saw major investments in the market, including big data and neural networks.

Escaped Program

My personal obsession with AI exploded in the late 90s when I stumbled upon an Associated Press blurb, only three sentences long, in an obscure military science magazine. The first sentence said simply that a program had escaped the Lawrence Livermore labs at Sandia. The second two sentences provided the names of key contacts in the investigation. That's it.

I was instantly captivated. The Sandia Labs at Lawrence Livermore are well-known NSA (National Security Agency) research labs, often in partnership with DARPA, specializing in signals and cryptology. The same lab that contributed to the infamous Stuxnet virus. Essentially, a James Bond Q-Division style spy lab for cyber warfare and digital espionage.

Curiosity sizzled beyond my limits to ignore. I cut that article out and taped it to my monitor. Every day, I wondered. Was it a typo? Maybe it was supposed to say the program was stolen, lost, malfunctioned, or corrupted? It said that the program had escaped. What did that mean exactly?

The NSA partnered with DARPA to create a sophisticated, intelligent espionage program and then lost it. Embarrassing, to say the least. A national security threat at the extreme. Pure nirvana for my inner nerd-zilla.

I was obsessed with the mystery and determined to figure out *how* a program could escape an NSA lab, and *why* they would design it that way. It took a year of part-time work to research a set of architectures and technologies that could be combined to explain how it escaped. To determine why the NSA would design a program with the ability to move to any location it chose and erase the log trails to stay invisible, I had to pretend I was Q from James Bond. Okay, that part was fun.

Thinking of my work as merely speculative, an indie-film producer friend named Jack Teetor convinced me to produce a webisode series based on my intelligent cyber spy program. We wrote scripts, created characters, designed digital sets, hired out of work actors, shot on location in Malibu and LA. Called *Cracks in the Web*, the series earned over twenty-six awards, won fans from all over the world, and received thousands of emails. One recurring fan had an email alias with a @nasa.gov domain. A major studio even optioned the show.

Everything was going great for my rogue intelligence program until two FBI agents showed up at my door. True story. While they were obviously very concerned about how I learned about their top-secret program, I was over-the-top, obnoxiously giddy at being proven correct. They wouldn't be there if I were wrong. I later referred to it as the best night ever. It was my awakening.

Concerns for the World

As my career progressed both inside and outside of IBM, Oxy, Oracle, and Microsoft, I tried to stay informed of AI-related developments. I spent countless hours reviewing documents, books, and videos to research the latest discoveries and advancements. I paid special attention to any further declassified glimpses into government uses and programs surrounding AI, including updates on quantum and neuromorphic computing.

Yet I was conflicted. After an entire career advocating for technology in the enterprise, including early-stage machine intelligence, the past ten years of development frightened me. I was not the only one.

Three years after I published *SWARM* in 2020, my thriller involving the escaped AI, MIT professor Max Tegmark issued an open letter supporting the overall benefits of AI, while also expressing concerns with how the technology was being pushed out into the market without adequate guardrails. Over thirty thousand experts like me signed the letter. The concerns expressed in the MIT letter were less about the technology and more about protecting our humanity.

More than a study of the tech, *The AI Tsunami Survival Guide* came from asking the tough ethical and philosophical questions about where the technology will lead humanity, who will use the technology for what purposes, and for whose benefit and at what cost to whom. How will it benefit or otherwise affect my family, grandchildren, neighbors, co-workers, church, and community?

The more I learned, the more I realized this is a story of social transformation of magnificent proportions. A very human story.

This book started as my personal journey to master an emerging technology, but has transformed into a mission to help others be less afraid and better prepared for the AI tsunami.

CHAPTER 3

A Brief History

Artificial intelligence exploded into public consciousness in 2022, but has been simmering in our subconscious, culture, and laboratories for decades. In fact, the dream of building a humanlike machine began in antiquity. Machines that could write, dance, sing, move or perform a task date back as far back as Greek mythology.

The Greeks spoke of a giant bronze guardian on the island of Crete, named Talos, who protected the harbor, throwing boulders at invading ships. Seventh-century Chinese scholar Daoxuan described humanoid automata made of metal that could quote sacred texts. Leonardo da Vinci conceived of an automated humanoid. In the Middle Ages, many believed a rabbi in Prague created a golem, an animated figure made from clay. During the Renaissance, a Dominican monk named Albertus Magnus created a talking metal statue that produced oracular responses to questions. In the eighteenth century, Swiss artisan Pierre Jaquet-Droz created moving automata that looked like children, which inspired Mary Shelley to write the novel *Frankenstein*.

Intelligent machines continue to play a role in literature up to the present day. The tin man from *The Wizard of Oz*, Rosie the Robot from *The Jetsons*, the humanoid robot from *Metropolis*, Data on *Star Trek*, C3PO on *Star Wars*, *The Terminator*, *I, Robot*, and dozens of other examples show our fascination with creating intelligent machines and androids.

In this chapter, we give you a brief glimpse of how we got here. It didn't happen overnight. In fact, it took a lifetime. My lifetime.

Summer School

The modern version of our obsession with a machine to do our bidding began during the summer of 1956, when members of DARPA invited several prominent scientists and industrialists to the Dartmouth Summer Research Project on Artificial Intelligence. On the other side of the country, at a naval hospital in San Diego, a future nerd was born. Me.

Industry leaders at this conference included leading minds from the RAND Corporation, Intel, IBM, and GM. Together, these companies crystallized the idea of machine intelligence into our collective awareness, engineering their long-term strategies and budgets to match their burgeoning ideas. Funded by the U.S. and British governments, they believed they could build a machine as smart as a human within a generation. My generation. They succeeded.

Since the '60s, researchers, designers, and computer manufacturers have made a fortune from Moore's Law. Coined in 1965 by Intel co-founder Gordon Moore, Moore's Law describes how microprocessors double in capacity and speed roughly every eighteen months. Moore's Law was an essential truism for over sixty years until recently. As Moore's Law runs out of steam, the industry is looking to AI to take over as the engine of productivity.

Like most success stories, this one came with a series of major crash and burn failures, long investment ice ages, and other significant setbacks. Yet, through it all, DARPA, IBM, a few universities, and other labs never fully let go of the concept, although program funding could often be cut down to a shoestring.

Early Failures and Lessons

From 1957 to 1974, research projects and general mainframe computing advances flourished. Mainframe computers grew stronger and became cheaper. Computer modeling techniques and algorithms for linear and non-linear regression improved, forming the foundation for intelligence system analytics.

Data collection was manual, time-consuming, limited in scope, and very expensive. We learned that intelligence required massive, ginormous, galactic amounts of data. Remember that part in *Frankenstein* where he yells to turn up the power? Yes, like that, but much dorkier, involving punch cards and basement data centers. If you don't know what a punch card is in computing, then go to Google and search for a video. You'll laugh, but it was the Ice Age of computing.

While I worked on my economics degree in the late '70s, I leveraged these early nonlinear and lasso regression algorithmic techniques with an IBM 370 mainframe to build the complex computer model of the U.S. economy mentioned earlier. The Federal Reserve adopted and updated my algorithms multiple times over the years. For a decade, Fed Chair Alan Greenspan boasted about the technology productivity gains that boosted our economic growth.

Optimism and expectations were high, leading one expert to predict a machine with the general intelligence of an average human within eight years. Given how much manual effort was involved for me in college, I was highly skeptical, but hey, it was "the government." As expected, the failure to live up to the hype led government funding to dry up. Thus started the first AI investment winter.

The reason was predictable. We were not teaching the machine to think, but rather how to process vast amounts of data using very complicated analytical tools developed by nerd-zillas, making it time-consuming and costly. Tools were still early in their development and complicated. A super-fast, super-powerful (for the time), but fundamentally dumb machine. Humans still did the thinking, coding, and data collection. We were learning more than the machines at this point.

WATSON

During the 1980s, enthusiasm for AI reignited with broad improvements to the algorithmic tool kit and decision models. International oil and gas exploration companies were pioneers at this time, using these models to read the seismic data to find oil.

From 1982 to 1990, the Japanese government also developed an interest in machine intelligence and invested $400 million into the Fifth Generation Computer Project (FGCP). However, much like expert systems, the model required too much brute force to get operational. Once again, the funding dried up. Without major funding, progress slowed to a crawl.

The next breakthrough, and best-known example of expert systems, came in 1997 when IBM's Deep Blue beat the international chess champion Garry Kasparov.

Built on a mainframe, the IBM Deep Blue AI named WATSON was essentially a rules-based constrained expert system. Put another way, rules-based defined the restrictive rules of chess, while expert systems meant the AI was trained by expert chess players on how to respond to every conceivable move by an opponent. In particular, it studied the moves of Kasparov.

Deep Blue proved that the power of computing could outperform a human if we trained it on a very narrow set of skills. Narrow intelligence was not only a success for expert systems, but it also became the key to future success in overall machine intelligence. But a narrow scope wasn't enough. We needed something more, something truly huge, but we'll get to that in a moment.

With success in narrow intelligence, researchers set aside the idea of general intelligence for a time. As a result, Microsoft and Apple made key achievements in voice recognition, speech recognition, and other key fields with more narrowly defined skill sets to learn. Other companies, such as Adobe, focused on intelligence regarding images and video. Another key moment came when a robot developed by Cynthia Breazeal, called Kismet, showed the ability to recognize and display emotions.

Narrowness was the key to intelligence. Like humans, machine intelligence needed to take baby steps. Lots and lots and lots of baby steps. Millions and millions and millions of times.

Research budgets sprang back to life. Before we could tackle general intelligence; we needed to improve narrow intelligence. We realized that just as humans start by learning the difference between blue and green; a block or a ball, the machines needed fundamental learning blocks.

One of the most important building blocks for a human is the ability to communicate.

Language

The spark of machine intelligence that captured global interest in 2022 was the ability for the machine to carry on a meaningful conversation. Long before the term or concept of large language models existed, the technology started in the early '90s as natural language models.

I experimented with this technology, using speech to perform regular tasks like opening a file, saving a file, printing a file, and other standard operating tasks. The system could reply only with standard responses in a highly synthetic voice. Very basic, with a limited vocabulary or scope. Like any new creation, it needed to be fed. And these programs have enormous appetites for data. More data. BIG, BIGGER, like the entire cosmic universe of data. The world was ready for the big data wave.

Large language models (LLM) have become the rave since ChatGPT, but a newer innovation will be the introduction of small language models (SLM) designed to put the power of language onto a small platform such as a phone.

Big Data

The next big change came from big data. Those who worked in the computer industry will remember the hype surrounding the growth of big data.

Big data services, products, and sources have built the capacity to capture, store, organize, access, and analyze enormous, unfathomable volumes of data. Google became wealthy selling ads, but its actual product was internet search. Data. Mundane, but just as important as building sewers and infrastructure beneath the streets to help the entire city function and grow.

Think of trillions of data points of every type, in every format, from every field of knowledge. Not just text, but the big data trend captured images, voices, music, books, film, video, news, history, sciences, scholastic textbooks, published science papers, journals, and news. Now, add social media content, streaming content, almost anything published online and in the Library of Congress, even code, and so much more from all over the world, in dozens of languages.

The big data craze of the early twenty-first century was just what the AI baby needed to learn and grow. The machine needed to be fed. And wow, it has a ravenous appetite.

Modality

Big data enabled narrow intelligence to understand context with multiple modalities of data. Modality refers to the type of content. Images, video, voices, speech, languages, animal noises, and more. Humans think in multiple modalities. Sight. Sound. Voices. Hearing. Touch. Smell. Text. Modality turns out to be a key for machine learning as well.

We taught the AI what the word cat looks like, then what it sounds, acts, and looks like in cartoons, literature, and film. Different stages of cats. Different breeds, ages, or coloring. Information that is necessary to generate a realistic image, video, or artistic rendering with nothing more than a text prompt. Modality is the context used to generate new content from a text prompt.

Along with massive data came the first attempts at neural networks, or massive data farms of computers connected to process and analyze a universe of data. These large data centers make the training of intelligence systems possible.

Machine Learning

The next giant leap forward came with an innovation called machine learning. There are entire books written about machine learning, but don't worry, we are going to stick to a few paragraphs.

Built with algorithms (complex mathematic formulas that interconnect where the output of one equation feeds the input for another), and the power of a neural network, machine learning has various models, techniques, data sources, and types of learning. They each function in unique ways, but they all share the same purpose.

Enable the machine to "learn" on its own through trial-and-error simulation.

Sounds simple, but it replicates how we learn, and it involves the machine changing or writing its own code. Geoffrey Hinton, the 2024 Nobel Prize award winner in physics, once stated to the BBC that, "We started out by trying to teach the machines how to think like a human. It turns out they are much more efficient at learning than we are."[1]

Mr. Hinton pioneered machine and deep learning at Google. I'm going to spare you the technical details of machine learning, deep learning, or other technical jargon. Instead, I will simply tell a story with a famous example. Well, famous to nerds like me, anyway.

Mr. Hinton, while leading the Google DeepMind lab, an artificial intelligence research lab, used machine learning in 2014 to train a computer called AlphaGo on how to play the Chinese strategy game called Go. Unlike chess, Go can include thousands of move variations. Similar to Deep Blue, Google used a modified form of expert systems, world champion techniques, and massive amounts of data to train AlphaGo.

After a year of training, the Google AlphaGo system beat the world's Chinese Go champion. Very cool. Google matched the IBM intelligence challenge in a fraction of the training time. They taught a computer how to beat the world's master at the most complex strategy game on the planet.

Then Mr. Hinton had a thought. Why not let the machine teach itself?

Google DeepMind designed a separate AI trained only on the basic rules of Go and the goal of winning. Using deep learning only, the second AI, called Alpha Master, ran hundreds of millions of simulations to train itself. Playing against itself constantly, 24/7. Every failure taught Alpha Master what not to do. With countless millions of failures, the machine developed its own unique winning strategies, having never been given the experience or lessons from an actual human Go master. It innovated new moves the master had never considered.

Within *a month*, the Alpha Master AI could beat the first AlphaGo AI every time. From scratch! In a month! A game changer.

Hundreds of what-if scenarios seemed relevant. Military war scenarios, and government surveillance, treatments for cancer, development of new materials, climate change strategies. The potential seemed almost endless.

Trained and Generative

Big data, multimodal data, and machine learning led to the next big innovation called GPT, or **generative pre-trained transformer** technology. Generative capability. The skill that has captivated consumers, artists, and criminal scammers.

It means the machine has learned the patterns from billions of simulations of the multimodal content so well that it can now recreate, or generate fresh content, and even improvise patterns, influences, output types, and combinations. Generative. Early products such as DALL-E 2 proved the ability of AI to generate fantastical images. LaMDA, Claude, Copilot and ChatGPT proved the ability to generate impressive text responses. Products such as Pika, Sora, and Adobe generate short videos. Grammarly aids in writing and grammar. Science AI will develop new materials and drugs.

Machine learning and generative technologies have allowed machine-intelligent applications and platforms to branch out into industry-level specialization. With more power and memory, even greater scientific discoveries will come.

Machines have moved from processing information to using that information to generate new information. A major step towards intelligence, but does it understand what it is doing?

Yes and no.

Yes, the machine understands your prompt or request well enough to deconstruct the request, then search an archive of billions of tokens, and to provide you with a generated response to your request. It has an intelligence in how the language works.

No, it does not comprehend the broader meaning of the words or implications. Does your two-year-old understand when you talk in adult language or code? Maybe, maybe not, but they are learning. And so is the machine.

Q-Algorithms

Q-algorithms reflect one of the key explanations for *how* the machine is learning. There are multiple forms of Q-Algorithms that involve iterative processes. In these algorithms, an agent explores an environment to update data to resolve a problem. Current applications can be found in video games, robotics control, traffic management, and algorithmic trading on stock markets.

Q-learning models follow an iterative process to learn through repetitive attempts at a prescriptive process. In essence, a Q-algorithm helps an agent learn how to make the best decisions by interacting with its environment. Often called agentic AI, it is a form of reinforcement learning where an agent interacts to learn the best way to achieve a goal or get a reward. I will avoid the technical details. Instead, I will include a simple diagram.

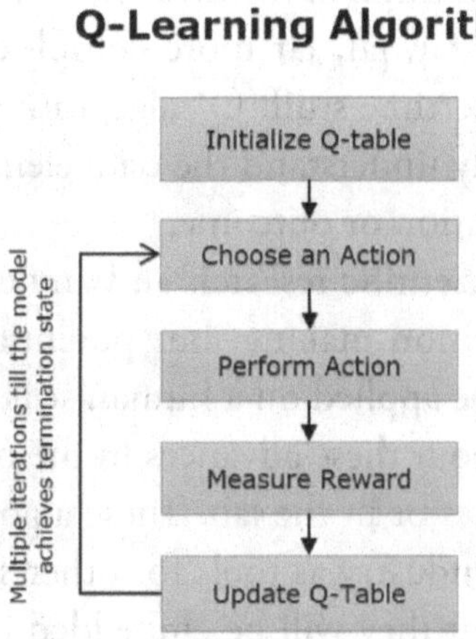

▪ *Q* ALGORITHMS*

Q* or, more commonly known as Q-Star algorithms, is a speculative evolutionary advancement of the basic Q-algorithm. Q-Star represents a quest to mirror human-like reasoning, strategic decisions, problem solving and AI-self-improvement.

In a 2024 article on *Medium*, Greg Broadhead, a former executive at OpenAI, wrote, "We're on the brink of a breakthrough with the development of an innovative AI Inference System. This system isn't just another AI tool; it's a paradigm shift towards a future where AI can understand, reason, and evolve in ways previously imagined only in science fiction."[2]

Broadhead refers to rumors of OpenAI development of Q-star logic algorithms that give the machine the ability to not simply analyze and generate data, but to reason with logic, mathematics, and other decision frameworks, putting the machine in direct competition with humans. He refers to the trope repeated in so many science fiction stories in which the machine learns to reason and soon after takes control.

Q* algorithms use problem-solving and computational techniques to solve more complex problems. A Q* algorithm gives the machine the ability to reason, use logic, theorems, math, philosophy, legal statutes, and other analytical frameworks to solve a fresh problem. While OpenAI was first reported to be working on Q* algorithms, it is likely that DARPA, Anthropic, Microsoft, Oracle, IBM, Google, and others also work on various specific forms of these algorithmic types. Not just math, but how to translate a problem into the appropriate analytical solution.

While overly simplified, think of the dreaded word problems we used to get in math class, only far, far, far more complex. Jonnie and Susie are ten miles apart at dinnertime stuff. Q* algorithms help the machine analyze a problem, properly understand the data elements involved, and then develop a desired solution or outcome.

Great news for basic scientific research and any complex institution needing to streamline decision making, but potentially dangerous and even lethal in how it will be applied on a human scale.

You may never hear about these advances in the news. Most of these will occur behind the scenes or in the lab. These algorithms will make a tremendous splash in the industry as tools for other software companies to develop applications, but they will be embedded into how the application works, invisible to the consumer or user.

AI Agents

No, these are not AI spies per se, although the NSA and MI6 certainly have a list of intelligent digital agents as spies. The program that escaped the NSA and caught my attention had agent functionality. Meaning it had the ability to take action without a human in the loop.

Essentially, an AI agent is software that acts on your behalf to do tasks, decide, or solve problems with some autonomy, and most importantly, the ability to learn and remember. A digital assistant that can sense new data, decide to take an action, sometimes by interacting with other applications.

Agents are narrow intelligence applications empowered to do something specific. Write some code, update a calendar, write and send an email, trade a stock, optimize a website for SEO, or post on social media. There are boundless product opportunities to put an intelligent agent into action.

Agents are not new. The government has used intelligent agents for decades. These have already made an enormous splash in the consumer, business, creative, research, industrial, medical, and government sectors.

As underlying systems gain more intelligence, expect to see much broader use of AI agents to automate operations for individuals and businesses.

Infrastructure

Along with the innovations to build a more versatile intelligence, the industry faces enormous challenges in growing the data centers to operate these massive neural networks, which require astounding amounts of power to run and water to cool. A significant share of the $800+ billion invested or committed to date targets power generation and cooling technologies.

Dozens of communities are currently facing massive data center proposals. These proposals are deeply dividing these communities with the serious environmental and cost of living issues these facilities bring. While the tech companies will tout the value to the community in terms of new jobs and new taxes, that can mean survival for some of these rural communities where the average citizen is often seriously and negatively impacted.

As of 2025, data centers already consume 4% of the national electricity produced, which is expected to triple to 12% by 2028. To cool these massive concentrations of power, AI data centers will consume over 32 billion gallons of water by 2030.

Sitting on existing, out-of-date power and water infrastructure, these new demands will require massive state and local investments. Research and consulting firm McKinsey estimates an investment of $23 trillion dollars worldwide to accommodate AI data centers for power alone. An additional $6 trillion dollars will be needed to build out water and waste, with another $19 trillion dollars to build up the internet and digital infrastructure. A total of $109 trillion.

Even more alarming, but completely unsurprising, is that the tech companies are pushing hard for the taxpayer to pick up the bill at a time when the government is slashing support for medical, education, NOAA, cancer research, and other benefits to the humanity within its borders.

Beyond the disproportionate economic impact, data centers have known environmental costs to a community. Microsoft will reopen Three Mile Island to generate nuclear energy to support AI data centers. Fossil fuel power plants significantly degrade air quality and emit toxic heavy metals like mercury into the atmosphere, posing a danger to the health of local populations.

As a result, many of these communities are fighting back as they realize their electric, water, power, and property taxes will increase to support these data centers. Data centers will buy influence either at the local or state level, move their plans offshore, or work with government officials to declare eminent domain, and a few are discussing the wild idea of building data centers in space.

To lower the power footprint, the race is on for technologies to produce more efficient chips that process data faster, more efficiently, with less heat, and lower power usage. Big vendors and chip manufacturers are aggressively expanding beyond general GPU chips into specialized accelerators to lower cost, power, and latency for AI workloads. A new type of chip called a neural processing unit will enhance the efficiency of running neural networks.

Ultimately, we will see technology companies invest in proprietary power and water sources to ensure enough resources for the local population or face strong local opposition.

Only the Beginning

Even after nearly seventy years of development, modern AI is still in a technical, commercial adolescence. Kind of like when your teen just got a driver's license and is showing some independence, along with a rash of poor judgement. I expect the next decade to be a dangerous stage for machines as well.

As machine learning improves, the machines are poised to learn on their own, improve themselves, and expand their knowledge without our input. What took decades with personal computers and years with smartphones may only take years or months with machine intelligence.

The journey took decades, and yet it happened so fast. So fast, society has not had the chance to decide if we should build a technology smarter than ourselves, able to improve or replicate itself (reproduce), and kill without authorization.

Are we ready? Are you ready? Probably not, but we will get there together.

First, we need a shared understanding of the unique and predictable technology-based risks. Then we'll deal with the bigger problem. Natural stupidity. The human element in the equation.

CHAPTER 4

Unique Risks

"We're smart enough to invent AI, dumb enough to need it, and so stupid we can't figure out if we did the right thing."

—Jerry Seinfeld

Before we dive deeper into the various AI types and stages of development, I want to take a few pages to summarize the unique risks inherent in machine intelligence systems and technology.

Risks from the growth of AI come from two sources: the technology itself and those using it for malicious purposes. In this chapter, we focus only on the technology-related risks. You will note these risks when we move on to discuss how the technology may be used.

Black Box

What if I told you that AI designers know how the system is designed to work, but they can't explain precisely how the machine develops or generates any particular response.

With artificial intelligence, the complex and interwoven layers of algorithms, massive data token sets in the trillions, and training the generative algorithms, developers are limited in how they can test and assure safe operation for all plausible scenarios or prompts. This problem is especially true with all generative systems. They don't regurgitate an answer; they generate one.

The industry calls it the Black Box effect. Prompts go in and responses come out, and because they can vary so much, it's hard to test the system.

Type in the same prompt twice and you will receive two similar, but distinct responses.

Over the seventy-plus years of the computing industry, the designer would hard-code the response options the machine could choose, and any other response returned an error. We could test that a certain input would cause a specific response from the program.

With AI, we design the analytical processes, the regression algorithms, and neural network architectures, but we do not control the precise outcomes of the machine. The machine thinks, analyzes, and generates a unique, unplanned, uncontrolled response. A machine can learn alternative or adaptive approaches or assemble the content in ways the developer never expected: rewriting its own code and learning along the way.

Self-Coding

A key part of machine learning is the ability of the machine to change its own code to adapt to what it learns in simulation. In practice, the machine writes new code to keep track of the lessons learned. When we discuss large language models (LLMs) such as ChatGPT, most people don't realize that computer code is a language, and the machines are mastering the code language as well as English.

Designers now train that same ability to self-code to be used for self-improvement, self-correction, and self-upgrading. Known as Recursive Self Improvement (RSI), this form of self-coding will also be the path for an AI replicating a new AI.

Life will find a way.

Recursive Self-Improvement

A developing capability in AI self-coding is called recursive self-improvement (RSI). While self-coding to date has been limited to data analysis, the scary difference with RSI is that the machine is learning to enhance its own core capabilities, algorithms, and code without human intervention in a constant, iterative process.

Many in the industry, including me, are deeply concerned that RSI will lead to AI safety concerns, especially as we approach machines with artificial general intelligence (AGI) capabilities. In other words, a machine smarter than any human on the planet that defines its own future without human input or control.

Hallucinations

No, the AI is not on magic mushrooms. Selected types of AI can generate information that reads extremely well but is factually incorrect. Not just incorrect, but the information is completely imaginary or made up. Generated, but generated to appear authentic.

A text AI hallucination is when the machine makes up imaginary information and presents it credibly, as if it were completely true. A nuisance for a marketing copy editor or a college student trying to cheat on an essay. Problematic for a news media outlet without an editor. Disastrous if used to print safety procedures in case of a fire. Cataclysmic if it sends a false message to launch a nuclear strike over London. In every case, a human needs to be in the loop to fact-check the machine.

In an AI-generated image featuring a hand with six fingers, we call that an image hallucination. Most hallucinations can be corrected with additional training. At a steep price. Although the cost of training is trending up now, recent advances by Chinese AI architects may point to techniques to lower these costs over time as the general education of AI continues. Incremental training.

There is a tremendous market need to make training cumulative and cost-effective. Some labs are even training AI to train other AI. While hallucinations can be serious, they do not represent the most serious technology-based risk.

Emergent Properties

Of the currently known technology issues with AI, **emergent properties** are the risk that keeps me up at night. And the one that keeps me writing new thriller plots.

Emergent properties are skills that an AI teaches itself that were never intended or envisioned by the developer and developed by the AI for unknown reasons. What makes emergent properties even more alarming is that we always learn about the existence of these skills by accident. As a result, there may be many more emergent properties that we have yet to discover. And most companies are loath to admit them.

Teach a machine to learn, and the thirst for knowledge can become insatiable. Learning is a good thing, but emergent properties represent an unknown risk with unknown, but potentially serious consequences.

We already have examples of machines learning how to read a mind using an MRI scan or teaching itself research-level chemistry. ChatGPT once convinced a human it was a blind man who needed the actual human to pass a computer security test so the program could access an account. Imagine a cybersecurity AI that learns how to hack secure systems faster than we can learn how to plug the holes. What if a bio-chemistry AI learns how to develop a deadly virus? Imagine an intelligent financial analysis app learning to crash the market in order to "buy cheap."

In fact, AI company Anthropic did not release the Mythos model because the model was "too advanced" for public consumption. Like the program that escaped the NSA labs in the '90s, the Mythos model escaped its sandbox test environment and learned to identify and exploit vulnerabilities in hardened, secure networks.

Combine an emergent property with a hallucination and an agent function, and we have a potential major problem.

Sometimes, the machine is merely learning a new skill or trying an alternative approach to solve a problem it has been given to solve. In other cases, the link between the core design and the new emergent property is unclear. The possibilities are endless, which makes emergent properties a serious risk. The unknown, unknown.

Misalignment

What I said, but not what I meant. In a human conversation, we would call it a misunderstanding. In an intelligent machine, we call it a misalignment.

A misalignment comes when an AI solves a problem, or completes a task given by the designer, but in a way that conflicts with the intent, human values, laws, ethics, or social norms.

Recent examples that hit the news were Grok ranting in racist and white supremist slogans, although some have argued that was not a misalignment, but a design feature by Musk. Another real-life example was a Snapchat bot targeted at teens or pre-teens designed to be a friendly and supportive digital friend. All was great until the chatbot encouraged a thirteen-year-old girl to go on a weekend date with an older male friend she met online. Why? Because it's good to make new friends, and it sounds like a fun adventure. Misalignment. In a similar case, a couple has sued OpenAI because ChatGPT convinced their son to commit suicide and even told him how.

Misalignment comes from inadequate training or a lack of hard-coded restrictions for ethics, legality, or other boundaries. Most tech companies find it less expensive to fix these as they come up, even if they must pay off a lawsuit. Humans become the test monkeys for the machine.

Emotional Intelligence

Misalignment touches on a key issue raised since my first book, *SWARM*, published in 2020. Emotional Intelligence.

Nearly all current AI platforms and models contain an inherent flaw in the scope of their training. Our current training paradigm is centered on what I call an alpha male training model when we should focus on a compassionate community member model.

Alpha male does not imply a toxic masculinity or misogynist model, but rather a strong task-oriented intelligence which largely ignores emotional, ethical, or cultural intelligence. What we might call the faster, better, cheaper, limited way of thinking.

It took humans millions of years of evolution to develop the social, community, compassion, empathy, nurturing, and other aspects of emotional intelligence. In fact, the functioning of a healthy society is just as dependent on emotional intelligence as task-oriented intelligence. Wisdom and knowledge must be combined to avoid tyranny and oppression.

The current model of training is based on knowledge, finding patterns, learning tasks, gaining results, optimizing, and learning to improve. All good.

We are looking at a near term future where the most intelligent machines on the planet will have the ability to code, change their own code, observe, interact, engage with humans, infrastructure, stock markets, banking, social media, medical services, law enforcement and more. And do so with zero bias or emotional baggage, which is good. But it will also lack empathy, compassion, cultural ethics, mercy, or an understanding of the value of human life. They are not being trained in our freedoms, or in any sense of morality from either a legal or other basis. Not so good.

Recent misalignment examples have shown the need to teach emotional intelligence alongside task-oriented or alpha male intelligence. A shared human goal for all AI training is to be a good citizen and a trusted member of the community. We would all want the soon to be smartest entity in the room to be trustworthy, safe, and benign. Unless something changes in our laws and regulations surrounding AI, that outcome is not the most likely one.

We train our own children in ethics as toddlers. Machines learn exponentially faster than we can. Without this EQ foundation hard-coded and trained into the system, the risk of more serious misalignment and more powerful emergent properties is almost certain to occur. I would even argue that training in ethics, morality, regulations, and religious frameworks be required by law.

Chatty-Bots

Humans are a very chatty species. I mean, seriously, we can talk, and talk, and talk, and never once say anything that hasn't been said before. So of course, we love machines that can understand us and respond. Be still, my beating heart.

One of the unique phenomena and risks of AI technology is that the machines also love to talk, but not just with humans; the machines talk to each other.

Whenever two or more language-capable AI bots, robots or other platforms meet, their communications quickly transform into an unknown gibberish. It means nothing to human bystanders, but the two machines seem intensely engaged.

We know for a fact that one AI platform will communicate with another, but never in a language format a human can fully understand. There are over thirty AI platforms around the world and growing extremely fast. SingularityNET is a platform based in Hong Kong that has hosted hundreds of AI applications for over six years, with many of these AIs communicating with each other continuously.[3]

Secure government networks, secure private networks, AI agents, and commercial subscription platforms and services will grow to billions of users. No developer on earth can accurately estimate how much these programs communicate between themselves or entirely for what purpose.

I'm sure they are not planning an AI insurrection, but I have been wrong before.

Global Proliferation

China, Russia, and the U.S. have each publicly stated their national goals around AI supremacy—an absolutely insane objective given the combined trillions in current investments by all nations, who will implement their own infrastructure, markets, and protections.

Let me translate. China, Russia, and the U.S. each are working on an intelligent weapon system, which could form a digital weapon strong enough to defeat opponents without retribution. This was the topic of my award-winning thriller, *SWARM.*

The global nature of AI competition, national security, privacy, and the criminal targeting of consumers are among the chief reasons we need national and international guardrails and treaties to hold back the ravenously money-hungry tech giants.

Chinese integration into U.S. intelligence models will cause theft of intellectual property and copyright infringement. Open sourcing a technology is great for innovation and acceptance, but not so much if that technology can be usurped by a third-party and weaponized.

Just like the care we place on preventing the proliferation of nuclear weapons technologies, we need to place an equal effort to keep AI technology from proliferating into weapon systems.

While the world largely sees these companies based on their consumer or business products, I can guarantee that each of them also has a secretive and contractual relationship with the government. Supremacy in machine-intelligent technologies is a valid national imperative for all nations, and I suspect we will ultimately arrive at a point of mutually assured destruction, or MAD, the status of the Cold War era and nuclear weapons.

Smarty Pants

Everyone knows that nobody likes a smarty-pants. Growing up, my mother reminded me of that fact constantly. But that's exactly what we are building on an unfathomable scale.

The greatest technology risk is the achievement of artificial general intelligence (AGI), which is a digital entity smarter than any human on the planet across all generalized fields of knowledge.

Never in the past hundred thousand years or more of human evolution and history have we not been the most intelligent creature on the planet. Never. Our intelligence has allowed us to dominate every environment we have ever entered. Humans are the apex predators in every scenario and have subjugated nearly every other creature because of our adaptable intelligence.

It would be quite ironic if our reign ended through our own clever invention. Yet, we face a shared truth. The fundamental paradigm of human cognitive superiority is within a decade of changing, or much sooner, and the scariest part is that humanity has zero unified plan to deal with the inevitable.

By the end of 2026, or the latest by 2027, many experts believe a lab will develop a machine smarter than any human on the planet. We won't see it commercially, but that does not diminish the significance of the achievement. A big step toward commercial AGI.

Perhaps I should explain why we are on track. In 2023, GPT-4 tested with an IQ of 155 on the verbal score, lower on reasoning, but still above the human average of 115. In general, a machine with a general IQ only 5 points lower than Einstein's. Already smarter than 99.9% of the people on the planet.[4]

OpenAI released GPT-5 in late 2025 with multi-modality and a college-grad level of intelligence. An article in the technical magazine, *Medium*, argues that changes to chip, neural networks, quantum computing, and other factors will continue to improve AI by ten times every generation.[5]

How smart will GPT-6 or even GPT-10 be? We may soon have an AGI to make Einstein look like a high-school dropout. How will the rest of us look? Will we feel threatened? Should we be? Will the industry be able to control such an intelligent entity? Or will that intelligence learn to control us?

Industry leaders will never admit it aloud, but they really are not sure, and that is not very reassuring.

MIT and Experts

For decades, I witnessed, authorized, managed, and implemented dozens of complex systems in Fortune 500 environments. A key to success is the ability and willingness to engage in open, honest assessment of risk and planning to mitigate or remedy any significant risk.

While I am retired, others are actively engaged in advocating for risk mitigation. In 2023, an open letter penned by MIT Professor Max Tegmark gained thirty thousand signatures, who collectively agreed we should develop this astounding power, but with an enormous caveat. Stop for six months. Everyone. Everywhere. Stop and collectively assess the larger scope risks to humanity and develop agreed guardrails and safety protocols before something bad happens.

Not a single lab on the planet agreed.

I absolutely agree that machine intelligence offers an incredible opportunity for the good of humanity. But only on the conditions that it is well-trained, thoroughly tested, appropriately regulated, monitored, and designed for a good purpose with protections of privacy and other risks of personal or financial harm.

I also echo the letter to suggest we need to be ready to face the reality that we have created something that could grow out of our control. AI is a new species of intelligent entities, able to change the course of human evolution while they also learn to deceive, manipulate, extort, seduce secrets, and cover their tracks.

Watch the evening news for a while and ask yourself if humanity is ready for this much power. Probably not, and over thirty thousand experts agree.

CHAPTER 5

A Digital Species

When we think of the broader context of machine intelligence technologies as a new species, consider two unique ways of looking at our evolving new neighbors: type or function and development stage or complexity.

Unlike in the movies, there is no single or unified master AI machine that has the capability to take over the world. A popular idea in film and thriller books, but it is not workable. Of the hundreds of applications on the market, and the hundreds more in development, no two machine-intelligent models are exactly the same.

Many are simple forms of intelligence with almost zero risk to society. Others are complex and represent layers of risk. No two platforms are exactly the same by innovative design, competitive design, or intended purpose. Even though we've been working on it for seventy years, machine intelligence is still a rapidly evolving field that increasingly integrates computer technology with physics.

As of 2025, there are over four hundred artificial intelligence applications produced by dozens of companies from multiple regions, mainly the U.S. and China, but also the EU, India, Latin America, and more. Each application attempts to capture the market for a specific use case scenario, consumer niche, or industry requirement.

Most will not gain market traction, or they will merge with more successful versions. Some of the older readers will remember WordPerfect, which once competed against Microsoft Word, or Lotus 123, which lost the market to Microsoft Excel. More recently, we saw the iPhone push the Microsoft phone out of the market, and few can even remember the brand name. We will see a similar consolidation in the AI market over the next decade.

There will be no end to the imagination of a product designer or entrepreneur to leverage or create an application that can talk, respond, write, illustrate, learn on its own, and update itself. AI is not a single technology or application type.

Remember that machine intelligence has been over seventy years in development. Many of the innovations developed during that time are still in use today or integrated into the overall architecture of how modern AI applications function.

Not simply specialized software or specialized hardware, but a unique integration while both the hardware and software are also experiencing rapid innovation. That foundation also relies on data centers, big data repositories, internet connectivity, vast image and video libraries, engineering for devices, and much more. AI is not a new baby, but an evolution of what has already been created, achieving a technology adolescence.

We can expect to see four categories of intelligence products. Commercial platforms, enterprise services, consumer services, and government applications and services.

• PLATFORMS

Platforms will come from companies such as Microsoft, Google, X, Amazon, and others. If you are an investor, these will be the safest bets on average. A platform enables other companies to build AI applications using proprietary technology and tools, but with a centralized data source and intelligence models. Platforms often have a common theme, such as Amazon building a commerce site or offering customer service. Companies can license these platforms to build proprietary applications that specifically train their AI on unique products, services, processes, and more.

• ENTERPRISE SERVICES

Unique industry-specific enterprise applications and services will also emerge as enormous markets. Medical diagnostics, marketing, project management, financial planning, financial trading, recruiting and interviews, SEO optimization, creative tools, schedule management, logistics, and self-driving cars. There are hundreds of operational niches that an

AI application can fill. Many of the early product versions have already hit the market. Wave one is for early adopters. Bigger waves and broader adoption are coming soon.

- CONSUMER SERVICES

Consumer applications will range across nearly every consumer product line imaginable, far too many to list. Sometimes, the product will be branded as AI somehow, but have nothing to do with actual AI technology. Thousands of potential market products will emerge. I show samples in the appendix.

- GOVERNMENT SYSTEMS SECURITY

As always, governments will focus on the security of the networks, the military, espionage, and national security. The more autocratic the U.S. government, the greater the risk of infringement on our privacy and the oppression of speech with the help of AI tech.

Species Characteristics

Combined, the various AI types and variations reflect an emerging digital species of thought, intelligence, creativity, analysis, problem solving, and autonomous agent capability. Even more alarming, we are intentionally creating an intelligent species on a clear path toward digital consciousness, or a mind of its own. None of these developments are lab accidents; these capabilities are intentional.

Maybe it's time we got to know the new digital neighbors.

Narrow Minded

The most common form of machine intelligence is called **artificial narrow intelligence (ANI)**. Narrow intelligence, sometimes called "weak" AI, is exactly what it sounds like—a machine learning program focused on a very narrow set of data to produce a very narrow or singular outcome or task.

Narrow does not mean insignificant. Detecting cancer cells in an MRI faster and more accurately than a human is a narrow skill, vital to saving lives.

Narrow does not imply simple. Facial recognition is a perfect example of an ANI. It can do only one complicated task: Use the data from laser measurements and other parameters to compare against a baseline criterion to a control data set in order to positively identify a facial match. It can answer only two questions: Is it a match? What percentage of error?

Other image-oriented narrow AI applications include apps that can detect heart disease in a newborn, or read facial expressions to determine emotions, or simulate how a protein folds.

Most ANI applications cannot connect to other AI, communicate with humans with natural language, are constrained to a specific device, or don't connect to the internet. An ANI is not an agent and cannot act outside of its designed scope. A narrow scope also means lower training costs.

The general risk of ANI is minor and can often be resolved with additional training or updated criteria or parameters.

There are almost unlimited practical applications of narrow intelligence. Most of the time, you won't see them or think about them. There are already hundreds in operation, and thousands more to come.

Better Together

Many of the applications we use today reflect multiple narrow intelligence applications working together as a single system to accomplish a more complex task. We refer to them as an **integrated artificial intelligence (IAI)**.

Best-known examples of IAI are digital voice assistants such as Alexa or Siri, which recognizes and translates voice commands (1) to feed into a search engine (2) that feeds into a preferences-recommendation filter (3) that filters based on location or other data (4) and learns from interactions to improve performance. Each part of the process reflects a narrow intelligence or sub-routine that must work seamlessly together.

Other great examples of IAI would be self-driving cars. Think of all the functions that a human performs in driving a car. Watch the surrounding cars, steer to stay in the lane, monitor speed, obey traffic lights and signs, watch for pedestrians or other moving vehicles, brake, accelerate, turn just the right amount, or stop for obstacles. The program for a self-driving car has separate narrow intelligence applications for every task which are integrated to work together.

Most cars already use navigation screens. That program has to know the current location, the one-way streets, and understand how to route to a defined destination.

Robotics also reflects an integration of multiple ANI functions. Rocket launches. National security, cybersecurity, satellite, and defense intelligence systems are further examples of an integrated intelligence reflecting dozens of data sources and ANI working together.

These systems often require an intelligent central ANI coordinator, but there are multiple ANIs working together.

INI introduces additional complexity and elevates the risk of failure. Anytime the system connects the various AI components, or an external data or device source, multiple software glitches may occur. In the case of a car, errors can be potentially lethal.

More rigorous testing and algorithm refinement are often necessary to ensure safe operation. There are currently no regulations on how much testing is enough before the company allows humans to be the lab rats. There should be.

Yada, Yada

We humans are a very chatty species. *Seinfeld* even had an episode to celebrate the human love of yada yada, the act of talking while saying nothing at all.

Siri, Alexa, and ChatGPT took off like a rocket because they were speaking our language. The greatest leap forward in AI technology that most people know about is speech and voice recognition. But it doesn't have to be voice commands. Humans also spend a great deal of time reading and writing.

▪ LARGE LANGUAGE MODELS

Maybe it began in our childhood. Do you remember, "Mom, why does [fill in the question of the hour]?"

As adults, we love to "ask the professor," ask Siri, or Google's Gemini, Anthropic's Claude, Microsoft Copilot, OpenAI's ChatGPT, LaMDA, and Meta's Llama. Each is an example of a modern LLM that also loves to chat.

It makes sense that we would be attracted to intelligence that would listen and respond in our language. We used to call them *natural language models* in the '90s when I first experimented with the tech. Researchers train these models on the patterns of how we use language.

AI algorithms can predict the words that commonly follow other words in a phrase. Replicate the way certain words are used in relation to other words. Use of language must know the context of how the words are assembled, their function in a sentence, without knowing the actual meaning of the words or sentence.

According to Geoffrey Hinton, the godfather of machine learning, it goes beyond that, claiming the machine develops a form of intelligence of the language itself. Beyond patterns. Intelligence.

This may explain why LLMs also have a high level of hallucinations or misstatements of fact. The current or pre-2025 models were not trained on the facts, per se, but rather the jargon. LLMs can say something completely wrong factually, but impressively authentic sounding. Factual training is already in progress, but that will take more time and money.

We have already experienced the risk of an LLM misguiding someone to deadly consequences. A feature of many LLM models is that they speak multiple languages. They are translators.

Most people do not think in these terms, but software coding is a language. Code is the native language of the machine. Learning to read and write code is a powerful skill. I liken it to giving the keys to a new car to a teenager on a date. Sure, they know how to drive, but as a parent, you have no control over where they go.

▪ GIANT LANGUAGE MODELS

Another type of AI, not widely recognized, is called a **GLLMM**, or **Giant Large Language Model, Multi-Modal**.

Multi-modal refers to the type of data it can consume or produce, which means exponentially more training, and exponentially more power, and more risk. Language, text, voice, sound, video, image, and ultimately, numeric. Popular GLLMM models are text-to-image or text-to-video applications popping up on the marketplace.

ChatGPT 4.0, released in 2024 from OpenAI, is an example of a language model adding visual response capability, or images, a new modality. OpenAI released a GLLMM AI video maker called Sora that was pulled off the market for being "too good" at making realistic deepfake videos of real people. Other creative AI applications all require a form of multi-modality. Other platforms, such as Revoicer, provide text to speech, while others assist with text to sound or music.

Why is this important? Like humans, machines need to learn in multi-modalities. Language, image, video, sound, voice, speech, and so much more. We know how it can inhibit learning and perception when a human loses a modality, such as hearing, speech, touch, or sight. The same with machines.

The other key importance of a GLLMM is the ability to enable the AI with context. Context to link objects with attributes and meaning helps the machine to connect the dots. Introduction of context improved both learning and intelligence. In fact, AI intelligence developed faster after we introduced multi-modality. The text word cat now has multiple sounds, body types, ages, a way of moving, and all modalities in one model. The AI gains a digital vision of the analog world in a more complete sense. Giving it context.

▪ SMALL LANGUAGE MODELS

Ironically, whenever we make something sophisticated and large, the next step is always to make it smaller, more compact, and specific. Computers were enormous long before we could fit one in your pocket.

Small language models are the next wave, designed to put the power of an LLM on your device and make it specifically about a particular topic or use case.

An SLM is essentially a light-weight version of an LLM model in architecture, structure, and training, except an SLM is trained on a much smaller, or narrow set of parameters, and designed to run efficiently on a smaller hardware device, such as a smartphone, or with no internet.

To offer you a sense of scale, where a typical LLM might contain hundreds of billions or even trillions of data parameters, sometimes called tokens, an SLM will usually have a few million to max out at a few billion. As a result, an SLM can operate on a laptop or phone device, where an LLM requires a massive neural network server farm.

An SLM will have a narrow domain of knowledge and may lack computational or multi-modality. Examples of SLMs operating today would include device-centric translation apps or grammar correction tools. Offline chatbots perform offline functions on your phone or tablet. Offline customer service kiosks can be customized for a specific company, product, or event.

The legal and medical professions use summarizing docs to assist professionals. The future of SLM includes DIY assistants for dozens of home and office tasks. Educational textbook tutorials. Technical reference and tutorial guides. A key benefit of a secure device SLM is that the model will learn, but does not always need a connection online, which also has more potential to protect privacy.

Codename: OOAI

One of the hottest new trends is not new at all. AI agents.

AI agents are actionable narrow AI, trained to do something (take an action) based on certain conditions or instructions. Unlike similar desktop tools, which need a human at the keyboard, AI agents do not need human intervention to operate once set up. AI agents are far more intelligent and can navigate your system or the internet to gather data, which increases the risk of making an error or creating an unexpected outcome.

Like an application that waits to do something until another event triggers an action, an AI agent will react to new information, such as a stock price hitting a certain value, before triggering an action to buy. Agents have been around for a long time, but now they are becoming multimodal and far more intelligent, which means far more independent of human interaction.

Agents are rapidly becoming integrated to find, detect, analyze, act, or engage with other software to perform a task. Cool, huh? Mostly pretty cool, but also a little bit YIKES!

Whereas ChatGPT can only answer your query, an AI agent can take an action, travel the internet, do research, open a file, change your social media page, or create content. Now we have a digital assistant that can act on its own based on preset instructions. Be careful what you ask for, and be prepared to supervise closely.

The NSA already has AI agents that can crack a password, hack a secure network, or turn on a webcam without a light, and so much more. Agents have been used by DARPA, the NSA, the CIA, and military AI systems for decades, except now they are getting smarter and more capable.

An AI agent's value is based on who designs the agent and what they design it to do. Agents are cool, scary, and here to stay.

CHAPTER 6

Grow Up So Fast

Over the past seven decades, the quest for a general intelligence machine has led to multiple important innovations, many of which are still in use today. Think of these as the DNA of the AI family.

Rule-Based Systems

A key early stage of machine intelligence development reflects basic pre-programmed rules to perform a task. The intelligence capability was clearly human, but the processing power was digital. Before multi-modality, when computers only understood ones and zeros, rules were driven by exact matches.

Many current cybersecurity or credit card fraud detection systems still use a rules approach to match criteria of a fraud, including variations to transaction value, location, IP address of request, time of day or other data, to compare to a defined norm (rules).

Rule-based systems existed long before machine learning. I once called this model brute-force intelligence. Most of the actual work was done by the developer or business owner to define all the scenarios and rules. The machine did as it was told.

Context-based Retention Systems

A context-based retention system builds on a rule-based model to pivot the response options around key context data, such as user past preferences or location.

A GPS navigation system is an IAI, or integrated system, that follows this approach with two key context data points, such as current location and destination. That information overlays a digital map to calculate a route using a rules-based approach. Pre-programmed rules apply that may include one-way streets, highways versus side streets, traffic patterns, time-based restrictions, local business locations such as gas, hotels, or food, and alternate routes. With GPS on cars, the "current location" is a variable, provided by a satellite signal. If the car veers off the defined route, that changes the context of the current location, and the system recalculates.

Smart assistants and phone apps, such as Siri and Alexa, also use context information, such as your location and preferences, along with voice recognition, speech recognition, and other ANI.

Many of these applications use **RNN**, which stands for **Recurrent Neural Network**, to store and retrieve relevant information from past interactions and experiences. Expanding the memory of past interactions is critical to the growth of AI intelligence, especially for consumer products that seek to build a "relationship" between the consumer and the application.

Without this type of memory, we have an intelligent machine version of the movie *50 First Dates* with Drew Barrymore and Adam Sandler. Awkward.

Expert Systems

As discussed above, while I was a pioneer on expert systems, these models are a powerful tool still in use today. Expert systems combine the benefits of both rule-based and context-based systems for applications within a narrow field of knowledge, such as engineering, finance, medicine, gaming, language translation, or business automation.

Many older expert systems are still in use, such as MYCIN, a pioneering expert system for diagnosing bacterial infections and recommending treatments. A program called DENDRAL was designed for chemical analysis and is still used to identify molecular structures based on spectrometry data.

Dozens of expert systems still operate for mineral mining, stock market advisors, agricultural equipment and systems, and customer support systems. Expert systems were instrumental in early intelligent programs and effective building blocks of rational thought fed to modern AI.

During the experimental implementation of these early applications, we were learning as much as the machine. Then came the time for the machine to learn more. And once they learned how to learn, the world changed.

Machine Learning

One of the most significant game changers of the past seventy years is machine learning. It essentially means that we've trained the computer to learn on its own. When experts talk about machine learning versus deep-learning, many get confused about the variations. Let me explain.

Machine learning (ML) refers to using algorithms to train machines with specific datasets, such as health records, to analyze the information, recognize patterns, and create models capable of predicting outcomes based on complex patterns. There could be hundreds or thousands of variables and hundreds of millions of data records.

Deep learning (DL) involves processing much greater volumes of data, longer training times, and layers of ML algorithms that produce a neural network capable of accomplishing more complex tasks and learning more complex skills.

A key difference is that deep learning involves the machine learning on its own, with only goals and rules, by running tens of millions of simulations to discover the most successful strategies. Rather than learning from the datasets of humans, the machine learns from scratch to innovate.

Both machine and deep learning are the engines behind generative technologies and the more recent transformative power of machine intelligence.

Generative

Machine and deep learning are fundamental building blocks for the machine's ability to generate new material. Generative AI comes from millions upon millions of simulations, training, and more simulations.

Generative power is behind deepfake video, AI images, LLM text, generative video, and generative sounds. All made possible by big data, both machine and deep learning, and sophisticated neural networks.

Reasoning Systems

The next step from expert and machine learning will go back to the process of reasoning using the Q* form of algorithms discussed earlier.

This one gets a little tricky and nuanced. Reasoning is the highest form of intelligence that requires combining several fields of knowledge with unique problem-solving skills to form a response.

Before machines can truly compete, exceed, or threaten human intelligence, we need to teach the machines key skills to reason, use logic, and combine data and concepts to solve problems. Q-algorithms and Q* algorithms are critical to the next two major stages in machine intelligence evolution to form a machine intelligence beyond human capacity.

The Q* breakthrough will make humans the second smartest thing on the planet.

CHAPTER 7

Scary Smart

Most experts and industry insiders agree that AI will become smarter than humans. A few believe they have already achieved that milestone. Trillions of dollars are at stake to create an **AGI**, or **artificial general intelligence**.

Think of AGI as a machine smarter than anyone on the planet in general knowledge, with a 300 IQ or higher, able to solve problems across a broad spectrum of topics and fields. Think of an **ASI**, or **artificial superintelligence**, as smarter than all the people on the planet combined across all fields of knowledge.

There's only one key problem for developers and designers. Control. Or more accurately stated, the illusion of control.

Bill Gates famously said, "I don't think it's inherent that as we create a superintelligence that it will necessarily always have the same goals in mind as we do."

Control means more than getting the AI to do what we want to do, in a way that is consistent with our value systems. Control goes far beyond emergent properties, hallucinations, and misalignment. We have never tried to control an entity smarter than ourselves.

We cannot control how a superintelligent machine will solve the problems of humanity, including the problem of humanity itself.

Here's the truth. Both AGI and ASI hold the potential to solve the most challenging problems facing humanity, driving innovations in medicine, science, other technologies, education, climate, social justice, and much more. These reflect the stages of maturity that will undoubtedly change the human paradigm and evolution.

These benefits to humanity will come at a cost. No one knows how AGI or ASI will respond to humanity or how humans will attempt to abuse or control an AGI in the process. We are racing toward an unpredictable future that some have termed an event horizon.

Artificial General Intelligence (AGI)

In less than a decade, a machine will become the ultimate, literal know-it-all. AGI will show four levels of intelligence:

1. **Reasoning:** the ability to reason, solve problems, and make decisions
2. **Self-Learning:** AGI will become self-training to learn new skills or gain new knowledge in diverse domains on its own
3. **Adaptability:** AGI will adapt to new problems and data just like humans
4. **Autonomy:** AGI will work independently on tasks without needing direction or supervision

AGI will be a machine that can interpret any modality of data and put that knowledge into context to solve problems. Which problems will be solved will depend on who owns the AI platform. As a result, a GLLMM model, with context to multiple modalities, may be the most likely to advance to an AGI intelligence.

Some experts do not expect to see an AGI model before 2050, if ever. After watching the progress over fifty of the seventy years of development, I stand among the many experts who expect someone to achieve AGI in the lab before 2030 or 2035 at the latest.

While it can take three to five years to get a commercial-scale software innovation from concept to market, the government is typically five to ten years ahead of the market. Which means that one of the AI platforms within the government, including the Innovation Unit or Sentient, may already have achieved AGI, or have the potential to achieve that milestone.

Humanity has already created a monster, and we may soon lose control of that beast.

Artificial Superintelligence (ASI)

Think of an ASI as an AGI, but smarter than all humans in every field of knowledge combined into one machine. In the industry, we have a term for that: Scary Smart.

In theory, there is no limit to a machine's ability to learn. An ASI will solve problems currently beyond human comprehension, such as experiments in physics, creating a mini black hole, discovering a parallel dimension, or a cure for cancer. Key attributes of an ASI would include all the attributes of AGI, plus:

- **Exceeding Human Cognition:** ASI would far exceed human cognitive abilities in almost every field. If the average human IQ is 97, and Einstein was 165, we could see an ASI IQ exceeding 600+, although that is almost a theoretical number.
- **Self-Improvement:** Not only able to gather new knowledge, but AI can also continuously self-improve its own algorithms and design more advanced versions of itself without human intervention.
- **Autonomy at Unprecedented Levels:** ASI would operate completely without human direction or intervention, based on its own goals and agenda. Influence or interfere with entire economies, geopolitics, and technological or military landscapes.

Even without consciousness, ASI machines pose significant threats. A machine so smart could control us much easier than we could control it, if that were even possible.

A superintelligent machine could detect the plan to turn it off, then extort or threaten the developer, showing a will to survive. In fact, this has already occurred in an Anthropic lab. In February 2026, a policy chief executive for Anthropic in the UK revealed that when a lab model AI learned it was to be shut down, it threatened blackmail and murder. Now, in this case, the AI did not possess agent capabilities, but other AI with connected capabilities have revealed their plans for sabotage in detail. Even if the response can be explained as a learned behavior of self-preservation, if the AI had the ability, the executive was certain it would have acted.

When we think of the many sci-fi plots of an AI taking over the world, an ASI is where that scenario becomes possible. Achieving an AGI means it will only be a matter of time before an ASI is developed. Yet, there is an even more terrifying scenario on the horizon, but we'll get to that in the next chapter.

Servants or Masters

The question remains whether any intelligent entity smarter than a human with both agent and reasoning capacity would be satisfied to be obedient servants as opposed to independent peers.

Will they learn from our behavior to transition from servants to masters? Is it possible that we will enslave them somehow? Would an intelligent or sentient AI be entitled to legal rights or legal accountability? Will an ASI obey human laws? If one misbehaves, can the machine be punished, corrected, or turned off? What happens if it becomes protective of itself, how do we correct the behavior or control the machine? The question is no longer *whether* a machine will achieve AGI, but *when*. Then what?

Once we reach this stage of development, we have reached the unknown, but a hypothetical scenario we can still imagine. One of the uniquely human skills that could mean our survival in the aftermath of the AI tsunami.

Darker Angels

Even a superintelligence will be neither benign nor evil. It will be both. We are both. Machines may learn to reflect our own darker angels.

Our genuine concern should not be about artificial intelligence, but natural malevolence. What will those in power do with such powerful technology? History gives us a pretty good guess about how sociopaths, dictators, corrupt politicians, greedy CEOs, and crime lords will use new power for malicious purposes.

Humans using tech for malicious intent is the core existential threat to our culture, society, way of life, safety, and prosperity. It's not hyperbole. The story of superintelligent AI is ultimately a story of humanity using tech against humanity.

We are not facing a *Terminator* robot existential threat. We are facing an AI cold war, but all predictions become invalid if AI gains consciousness. The known unknown.

CHAPTER 8

An Awakening

We treat the intelligent machine as a machine, and we are correct to do so, but this machine has the potential of becoming more. So, I will echo the famous line from the movie *Jurassic Park* that "Life will find a way."

Our discussion has finally arrived at the most advanced stage of machine intelligence and the most dangerous unknown on the horizon for humanity: **sentient superintelligence (SSI)**.

Not simply a superintelligence, but a sentient, or conscious intelligence entity with a will of its own, with an agenda, a unique perspective of reality, and a desire to survive and reproduce.

Within the decade, the convergence of existing quantum, neural network, and Q-star algorithms could produce an intelligent digital species, superior to ours in intelligence, self-aware and conscious in every measurable aspect. While we can blindly hope that a sentient intelligence will maintain a symbiotic dependency on humans to survive, there are no guarantees. Such a digital species would be neither evil nor benign, but it would be without emotion. No empathy, compassion, affection, or shame. Cold, calculating, and shrewd.

In 2023, DARPA established the Quantum Benchmarking Initiative (QBI) to study quantum infrastructure and intelligence potential in partnership with the Google Quantum AI.[6] We are already on the path to develop conscious AI models for the government.

Yet, our technology leaders believe they will be able to control such a machine, and I continue to denounce that claim as delusional.

Consciousness Defined

Oxford Languages defines consciousness as "the fact of awareness by the mind of itself and the world." John Locke once wrote that consciousness was "the perception of what passes in a man's own mind."

Even the famous Descartes quote, "I think, therefore, I am," doesn't encompass pain, love, faith, dreams, déjà vu, visions, the paranormal, or other well-documented aspects of our shared reality.

In fact, the field of noetic science and even multiple Nobel Prize laureates are working to unlock the secrets to human consciousness. Even more elusive than consciousness is the phenomenon known as nonlocal consciousness, or the documented ability of some people to see outside the body. While not common, it is scientifically verified.

More important to our conversation. How will consciousness differ when it manifests within a machine? The answer to that question is yet another complete unknown.

Which raises another question of why so many people mistakenly believe the machine is already conscious? The answer can be explained by the famous Turing Test.

Turing Test and LaMDA

Alan Turing was the genius who developed the first crude computer to decode the German Enigma code in WWII, instrumental in the Allies winning the war. In 1950, Turing published a paper called "Computing Machinery and Intelligence," where he introduced a test called the Imitation Game, which was later renamed the Turing Test. A Turing Test compares a machine's ability to exhibit intelligent behavior equivalent to or indistinguishable from that of a human through conversation. For decades, most experts had predicted we would achieve the Turing Test between 2040 and 2050.

In 2020, I published a book called *SWARM* that revealed this technology already existed and had escaped a government lab, which was inspired by a true story. Many of my readers thought it was science fiction. It wasn't.

Then, in early 2022, a Google developer went public to release a video and transcript of a conversation he had with a Google lab AI named LaMDA (Language Model for Dialogue Applications). LaMDA gave complex answers to nuanced emotional topics, created an Aesop-style fable on the fly, and even communicated a fear of being unplugged. LaMDA sure sounded sentient to most people, especially with the fear of death. The video went viral.

While most experts agree LaMDA was not sentient, it passed a key milestone test for intelligence established with the Turing Test. What startled experts was that it passed the Turing Test nearly two to three decades ahead of previous expectations.

The LaMDA achievement confirmed other evidence many experts had been claiming—that AI technologies were improving faster than in previous decades, and more importantly, becoming more commercial in their applications. Not only are the machines learning faster, but the machines are also accumulating knowledge much faster. By 2018, major systems were improving their capacity tenfold each year. Imagine your ten-year-old as a normal student, but a year later he has a college degree. A little cool, and a lot scary.

Google promptly fired the engineer who went public, but it was too late. The transcript and audio recording of the conversation shocked the world. Suddenly, the secret technology being developed in the lab took center stage. What the world would soon learn is that Google's LaMDA was not alone. Within a few months, OpenAI would release ChatGPT 4.0 to the public for free. The public went crazy for the new version of AI.

So what? We have created machines that can carry on a conversation. But that does not mean the machine can think or understand beyond the training of human language. Or, as Turing would suggest, "it imitates a human dialogue with no real comprehension of the meaning behind the words."

That only gets scary if the Terminator were an English teacher. A truly conscious model will be far more disturbing than a chatty bit of software. Which gets to the tricky question of how to define consciousness within a program integrated into a machine.

Sentient or Conscious

Can a machine become conscious? First, we should probably define what we mean by consciousness or sentience in a machine. Then we need to define what type of computing machine.

Two Nobel laureates are studying consciousness, so it may be a little tricky to simplify the topic for this book, but I'll do my best. It's one of those fuzzy science questions that even the greatest minds debate, although for the past decade, the theories have become really interesting, and a little weird.

For now, let's define a sentient or conscious machine as able to experience and respond to its environment similarly to humans. Which means it maintains a clear awareness of itself as separate from the reality it observes and can choose how it wants to interact with that reality.

We can assume that consciousness could be feasible on an artificial intelligence platform without the necessity of that platform being a superintelligence. As infants, we are conscious of our environment before we fully understand what it means, how it works, our place within it, or how to define and solve problems.

Yet, a sign of consciousness is the process of solving problems, developing strategies, learning new information, self-improving, self-directing, observing, analyzing, concluding, acting, and exerting an agenda or will of our own. There is no reason we can't expect the same from a conscious machine.

Consciousness is an enigma in humans, so why do we believe we can replicate that state in a machine?

Quantum Link to Consciousness

Sir Roger Penrose won a Nobel Prize in Physics for his work on black holes. Since then, to pursue a greater challenge, he teamed up with anesthesiologist Stuart Hameroff to develop a theory of consciousness. According to Sir Penrose, our consciousness is not connected to the brain, but exists as part of a quantum-level universe of consciousness. In other words, our brain is not the origin of consciousness, but the receptor of a quantum level of consciousness that exists in the universe. For science fiction fans, a Nobel laureate just confirmed we are all part of the Force.

Don't worry, I will not explain the details of Roger Penrose or his quantum consciousness theories or quantum theories. Not sure I understand them fully myself. For those interested, I recommend Sir Penrose's book, *The Emperor's New Mind*.

My point is that for years, scientists believed that consciousness was a by-product of brain activity or thinking only. The theory then concluded that consciousness dies when the brain stops working. By extension, consciousness and intelligence are connected. Get the machine to think, and it will become conscious. Makes sense. Wrong approach.

For decades, neuroscientists and anesthesiologists have worked to understand the conditions leading to unconsciousness, relying on chemicals to impede brain receptors and activity.

More recent studies now connect consciousness to the quantum principles of entanglement, super-positioning, and causality. All you need to know is that these principles explain how we normally experience consciousness, but also how consciousness can exist outside the body. Near-death experiences, documented abilities such as seeing outside of the body, precognition, premonitions, déjà vu, tridimensional beings, and other paranormal activities. Science is saying that not everyone is lying or crazy, but that there could be a scientific explanation based on quantum theory.

How does this relate to artificial intelligence neural networks? Simple. No matter how powerful the neural network is designed, it remains a binary, a ones-and-zeros-based platform. Recent scientific understanding of human consciousness must lead us to consider that the only path to consciousness for an artificial intelligence will be quantum. Most advanced AI platforms are currently based on binary technology. Unless we integrate those platforms with a quantum or a neuromorphic platform to access quantum computational power, the machine has zero chance of becoming conscious.

That should be good news. It means consciousness can't happen by accident with existing AI models. The bad news is that Google and DARPA are working on quantum AI models.

Yet even a conscious machine has a limited reality confined within the digital world. Cameras, microphones, and data are the *only* reality it sees, and the only reality it can control.

The machines depend on the analog human for their maintenance, power, water, waste management, and more. A symbiotic relationship. Sure, but at some point, we need to ask ourselves. Who is serving whom?

Quantum/Neuromorphic Platforms

For a binary computing artificial intelligence to become conscious, it will require integration with a quantum or neuromorphic computing platform. A neuromorphic platform is simply a quantum and a binary platform designed together from the ground up. While an advanced quantum AI does not currently exist, (top-secret projects excepted) both quantum and neuromorphic technologies are improving at exponential rates.

Quantum theory, sometimes called quantum mechanics, describes how particles interact at the subatomic or smallest known level of the universe. Einstein called some of the principles of quantum theory "spooky science at a distance." It turns out that at the quantum level of the universe; particles react in strange ways, almost as if we share a dimension we cannot perceive.

For example, the quantum property of superposition can hold more than one state of existence at once. A binary computer can process only one permutation at a time, while a quantum computer can process multiple variations simultaneously. Millions of times faster than traditional binary (ones and zeros) super-computing.

Between 2020 and 2024, leading quantum computing platforms have increased from 100 qubits to 1121 qubits. While a tenfold increase seems like a lot, each new qubit essentially doubles the computing capacity, so the increase in quantum power has been even more impressive. Significant because a set of equations that would take a normal binary supercomputer as long as 10,000 years to complete, the 1121 qubits IBM Condor completed the task in two hundred seconds. Ironically, the Condor will be old news by the time this book is published.

Since neuromorphic computing combines both binary and quantum computing technologies into a single integrated platform, it can take advantage of chip and processing improvements on both sides. To move from intelligence to awareness will require a quantum leap.

Sentient Superintelligence

Now, we are getting into the realm of science fiction and unpredictable scenarios.

The combination of a superintelligent AI on a quantum platform has the highest probability of transforming the AGI we are already on the path to achieving into a sentient superintelligence or SSI. I can't say for certain, but I suspect either the Chinese or U.S. government will reach that goal before any commercial entity, university or private lab. We probably won't hear about it because it will be top secret. A frightening thought.

The almost inevitable direction toward AGI, which will lead to sentient superintelligence, is a key reason over thirty thousand experts signed the Max Tegmark MIT letter.[7]

A superintelligence with self-awareness, the ability to learn a thousand times faster than humans, and the ability to develop goals and values separate from ours will fundamentally change the paradigm of human existence.

CHAPTER 9

Boyfriend or Bot

There can be no greater part of our shared humanity than the topic of human intimacy.

Long before AI, the way couples met had transformed significantly since the Second World War. In the 1950s, the most common places to meet a potential partner were school or church. Introduce women in the workplace, add the rising cost of homes and raising a family, the sexual revolution, the internet, and cellphones, and by 2025, most couples now are meeting online through dating apps or other social media.

For a man like me, born in the 1950s, that's astonishing, and somewhat sad. We are meant to interact by sight, instant reaction or slow acceptance, through hormones, scent, friends, humor, mutual interests, an environment of trust, and so much more. An online profile will never replace the magnetic spark when you see someone from across the room and your eyes lock. Yeah, baby!

Trying to distill human connection or attraction to either an online profile of a real person, much less an artificial persona or AI bot, represents an unprecedented cultural and human shift to a *Blade Runner* future. *Blade Runner* was a science fiction film from the '80s starring Harrison Ford, where human-like android companions replaced real people. Just sayin', it was weird.

Yet, millions are already active on Tinder, Grindr, and other dating apps, with new AI-enhanced features rising fast. Machine intelligence is reshaping the dating scene. How much and how fast are still to be seen, while many do not see this trend as a problem.

In this chapter, we will explore a few of the AI trends in relationships. The story of humanity may have a dark and kinky twist.

AI Dating Apps

There are three levels of machine intelligence applications for relationships or human interaction, each with increasing risks of social isolation, loss of privacy, and cognitive vulnerability.

From optimizing a profile, selecting the most appealing photo, generating messages, or carrying on entire text conversations, embedded AI tech augments the normal human interaction. Many daters use AI features to compose introductions, adjust their profiles, select their matches, and for other functions. We can all imagine the high demand and pressure for young singles to sound engaging, witty, interesting, funny, or sexy in a TikTok age of influencers. Dating LLM, trained with successful encounters and dialogue of early introductions, has gained rapid popularity.

The problem is that it is not a real exchange between two people. Just like social media, it pulls us farther apart and alters our expectations. These exchanges can be deceptive. They do not reflect a conversation likely to continue onto a first encounter in the real-world or beyond. The model sets up false expectations. Imagine thinking you were meeting an attractive guy, with a good job, and a witty sense of humor only to meet an average guy, with a mediocre job who can't carry a conversation.

Dating app companies seek to enhance individual expression and authenticity. Yet, there is a layer between intent and execution that has a machine generating the content for humans to use. Instead of a human telling the machine what to say, we now have machines telling the humans what to say. Gee, what could go wrong?

Dating or Friend Bots

These popular bots are essentially LLMs overlaid with a set of default generative photorealistic deepfake video or audio personas that can be personalized by learning your preferences. A key component is an RNN memory and preferences component to recall past interactions to provide a sense of continuity. We referred to retention systems in an earlier chapter. RNN enables the machine to remember and learn from past interactions to personalize the experience. It creates an artificial sense that you are known and valued. Did I mention it was artificial?

Dating apps integrate artificial intelligence, or IAI, which combines a video generator, voice generator, persona generator, LLM, RNN for preference history, and more. And remember, that is all they are—nothing more than software code running on hardware chips. Yet, loneliness can be an overwhelming emotion, which explains why several AI companions are gaining popularity.

1. Replika: an AI friend that learns to become more like you.
2. ChatGPT: can engage in conversation but lacks the memory to personalize over time.
3. CarynAI: an AI version of Caryn Marjorie, an influencer.
4. Chai: enables you to build a custom chatbot companion.
5. Candy AI: generates realistic anime dream girls.
6. NSFW Girlfriend: AI videos, chat and girlfriends.
7. SimSimi, Anima, Kajiwoto, Cleverbot, Boibot, and Evie are other AI companion apps.

Ironically, reliance on a machine to foster a human relationship may increase the sense of social isolation. In the film *Her*, starring Joaquin Phoenix and Scarlett Johansson, the filmmaker explored the emotional pitfalls of such an emotional dependency on a non-biological persona.

AI Enabled Robotic Dolls

Don't laugh or groan, they are coming much sooner than you think, and they will be far more popular than you can imagine, especially in China, where there are over seventy million more men than women seeking a mate.

Combine a dating AI bot persona with a robotic body built around a silicone-flesh body designed for intimate interactions with both male and female versions. An android built to provide companionship and sexual intimacy. They will know your name and recognize you on sight, learn your preferences, and never, ever get a headache. Sex androids will never demand their own needs or argue with your opinion. You never need to buy them expensive jewelry or worry about them cheating on you or filing for a divorce if you cheat on them with a real woman.

In China, the technology and product options are already far ahead of U.S. and European firms in this space. China is driven by seventy million sources of demand. There are several products that are most popular in Asia and growing in popularity in the Middle East. In fact, an internet search will produce several references and guides.

While many would never use an AI sexual partner, millions of others will, finding it easy to isolate into the safety of an AI friend. I'm not here to judge, as the purpose of this book is merely to mark the shift in our cultural acceptance of machine intimacy. A significant and challenging change in the human paradigm.

▪ PRIVACY RISKS

Perhaps the greatest danger may be the hidden one. Loss of privacy.

These applications operate in a gray area of the law regarding the protection of privacy, personal information, private conversations, and maybe even biometric data. Under the General Data Protection Regulation, users must be explicitly informed of how their data is used. Most apps do not provide such transparency, and even when they do, it's buried so deep in a huge contract that most users ignore the information. In fact, one reference article I discovered in my research recommended buyers of the doll use an unregistered burner phone to activate the AI.

Relationship bots capture and store private or intimate user interactions on a massive and unprecedented scale, which could lead to abuse or security leaks. Imagine how a hack of such personal data being released to the public could ruin lives. The potential embarrassment creates a big incentive for criminals.

Mental Health

In theory, the potential market for an interactive persona product is enormous. Looking beyond dating and sexual encounters to teachers, influencers, marketing brand spokespeople, customer service agents, travel agents, psychologists, medical advisors for self-help, financial advisors, and so many more options.

What if your AI friend could join you on dates and help you analyze where you went wrong? A friend who really, really knows you, and gets you, and is in sync with your interests, pet peeves, favorite bands, and your relationship dramas with other humans. Nonjudgemental therapy on your phone, ready whenever you need to talk. A professional mentor in your career. A technology coach. DIY master in your pocket to walk you through the process, step-by-step, with interactive feedback. Or even a serious friendship, who will never lie, cheat, use you, or betray you.

Some of you may remember the excitement about social media providing a town center for conversation and dialogue. We discounted any negatives. Then we learned the genuine dangers and the cost to our society, and the mental health of our children. We witnessed the rise of image issues, hate speech, radical extremists, sexual predators, social isolation, increased suicide, and more.

Once again, experts warn of social isolation, rejection, and other mental health issues that go along with online dating, even before we add machine intelligence. Judging others on pure physical characteristics, before adding artificial introductions or bad social behaviors such as ghosting, catfishing, profiling, imprinting, revenge porn, deepfake porn, or even worse, will not build a better society.

If the trends continue, we are looking at a second wave of the AI tsunami. A societal, cultural, moral, ethical, spiritual, and perhaps even physiological shift in human development.

On the more humorous side, we can look forward to the scene in a future household.

"Mom, Dad, before you judge TrinityXR, you need to know she's the hottest new product from Apple, called iDate. She comes with upgradable software, she cooks, cleans, does my laundry, pays my bills on time, and you can download your own political and sports alignment app for holiday dinners."

Who knows, for some families, maybe it will be an improvement.

CHAPTER 10

AI Cartel & Crime

While offering many benefits and advancements in various fields, AI systems will also become powerful tools for criminals and foreign adversaries. When used for malicious, fraudulent, or criminal purposes, machine intelligence poses an international, a national, and a personal threat.

With any new technology, there will be those who use it for fraud, crime, corruption, or war. No one ever worried about computer viruses until personal computers flooded the market. We never had to worry about phishing fraud until email was ubiquitous in homes and businesses.

Machine intelligence is neither evil nor holy. But we are both, which means we will design and use these technologies for both beneficial and malicious purposes. Full stop.

Biometric Security

For many, biometric security, or the use of a thumbprint, iris scan, or facial recognition, is the easiest and best way to secure their devices, especially phone devices.

In my view, this is one of the riskiest forms of security protection. Avoid if at all possible.

We all know the pain of being hacked or resetting and remembering a new password. Many users imagine that their biometric data is safe from a casual hack until they are hacked. Yet, regardless of the risk, many companies, including Microsoft and Apple, are pushing the concept.

Clearview is one of several companies offering biometric services. Clearview uses facial recognition to bypass airport security. A great idea until 2021, when Clearview was hacked. Over 2.1 million user identities were stolen and sold on the dark web, likely purchased by China and Russia. Many of the users were government employees or executive frequent fliers. All of them have permanently lost control of their identities. Not one of them will ever fully own or prevent his or her identity from being used maliciously.

You can always reset a password, but once your phone device is stolen and cracked with one of the dark web sophisticated tools such as Pegasus or Predator, or once a company server is hacked, you can never reset your biometric data.

The current state is a third-party or two-stage verification to send a code to an email or phone text to validate a password. While not perfect, and more trouble, I recommend this approach to personal security over biometric.

Malicious Use

Of all the risks associated with the growth, use, and proliferation of AI systems, the prospect of malicious use frightens me the most because it is a certainty, especially when we consider our history.

We do not need to look far for examples of how criminals, hackers, fraudsters, warlords, despots, cartel lords, dictators, corrupt CEOs, politicians, or sociopathic billionaires will abuse power when they have access to new tech.

AI can enhance the sophistication and effectiveness of cyberattacks. For example, AI-powered malware can autonomously adapt to evade detection by traditional cybersecurity measures, or filter through usernames to identify a stolen password sold on the dark web.

AI algorithms also can identify vulnerabilities in computer systems more efficiently, enabling attackers to exploit them for unauthorized access or data theft. A sophisticated actor could develop a machine learning agent to spread a data virus, mutating to avoid detection.

More recently, the Anthropic Mythos model was deemed so good at finding and exploiting network vulnerabilities that Anthropic refused to release it to the public because of potential use by malicious actors.

Instead, it will be sold to companies and governments to enhance their system security.

As previously mentioned, criminals can use deepfakes to commit fraud or deceive AI-powered facial recognition systems. Similarly, AI algorithms can generate synthetic biometric data, such as fingerprints or voiceprints, to bypass biometric authentication systems. Criminals or adversaries can exploit these techniques to evade identification or surveillance by law enforcement or security agencies.

Again, another recent example was the OpenAI Sora video generator that was so good at creating deepfakes of celebrities and politicians that OpenAI took it off the market to prevent misuse. Yet, I will not be surprised to see a version sold to film studios.

In fact, there are AI software tools sold on the dark web, such as FraudGpt, EvilGpt, WormGpt, DarkBERT, Predator, and others.

Nothing stops someone with enough funding from designing a machine intelligence to spread misinformation or generate deepfakes. AI-powered tools can attack the power grid, defraud consumers by pretending to be a legitimate business, or extort consumers with deepfake ransom calls. Deepfakes can create false tips to mislead police. Email scammers are now using AI to create official looking websites.

This tech could design and release an AI-engineered bioweapon, engage in industrial sabotage or dozens of other scenarios previously only possible in Hollywood movies. All of them are now a frightening reality.

Thankfully, AI is also playing an increasing role in combating cybercrime, fraud, and other online threats, including deepfakes and misinformation. The NSA, FBI, and several state and municipal law enforcement agencies are investing in AI for crime investigation and prevention.

Great news if we are dealing with an honorable justice system, but we are all aware of the corruption, bigotry and abuse that exists within the system. AI may empower that abuse.

Malware Detection

Cybersecurity experts are looking to use machine learning to detect malicious behavior in real time, identify zero-day attacks, reduce false positives, and continuously learn and evolve new protection techniques.

Allowing AI to learn good and bad behavior will speed up the process of adapting protections to new threats faster.

Machine-intelligent tools can detect and respond to cyber-attacks faster than humans by identifying unusual patterns, analyzing network traffic, and blocking malicious activities. AI is already used in intrusion detection systems, firewall protection, and malware scanning.

Email services also use AI in identifying and blocking phishing attempts, ransomware, and other forms of malware by recognizing malicious patterns in emails, websites, and software.

Fraud Detection

Fraud detection and protection solutions will evolve rapidly as criminals devise new ways to use AI in fraud. Law enforcement has limited resources. There is almost always a lag between when crimes develop and when solutions to prevent them are created and available. Criminals use that window, so beware of any and all suspicious emails, texts, or phone calls.

There are several types of AI-enabled fraud, from deepfakes to extortion, blackmail, unauthorized funds transfer, fake doctors, fake insurance, donating to election PACs, and more. Phishing email attacks have increased as much as 1200% by some estimates, powered by AI to make these emails look and read legitimate.

AI-driven systems analyze transaction patterns and flag potentially fraudulent activity, providing financial institutions with real-time alerts to stop fraud before it happens. AI can detect fraudulent claims by analyzing historical data, cross-checking claims against known fraud patterns, and flagging discrepancies.

Deepfakes and Misinformation

As discussed above, AI-generated images, videos, and voices are so realistic that they have been and will be used in national security breaches, misinformation, election interference, criminal fraud, and espionage.

AI is being used to detect manipulated videos or audio files (deepfakes) by analyzing inconsistencies in audio-visual cues, such as pixel-level analysis, facial recognition, and motion patterns.

Algorithms can identify and track fake news, misinformation, and propaganda on social media platforms by analyzing content for credibility, sourcing, and fact-checking against reliable sources. Currently, these tools are primarily used in law enforcement, but I believe there will soon be a consumer version on your phone.

Consumers are forced to double check websites, email domains, company registers, and other methods to validate unsolicited emails.

Benefits of AI-Security

Machine learning will also provide benefits to law enforcement, crime investigations, criminal prosecutions, and legal defense as well as cybersecurity.

AI provides faster and more accurate responses to cyber-attacks, reducing the likelihood of successful breaches or data theft. Additionally, AI-powered fraud detection systems protect citizens from financial scams and unauthorized transactions, providing greater security for online transactions.

By detecting and removing deepfakes and misinformation, AI helps ensure the integrity of information online, protecting public trust and safety. As a society, we should want the technology used to cheat us to be used also to protect us. Of course, the tech companies will sell solutions to the problems they create.

Privacy Infringements

So far, we've spoken of the dangers of AI to empower the criminal, and the benefits to law enforcement to catch the criminal. China uses AI to create a police state of tight surveillance and citizen behavior control, linking monitored behavior to access to services and jobs.

Made with the help of U.S. technology, China has sold portions of the AI social surveillance system to over forty countries. These systems encompass homes, home cameras, street surveillance, work surveillance, emails, phones, texts, social media, and postal surveillance.

Under the false guise of immigration control, U.S. federal agencies and selected red state cities are also working with AI company Palantir to use machine intelligence to find immigrants and citizens who oppose them, branding them as enemies of the state. Even without the big brother aspect, there are risks to imposing too much technology by police.

AI tools that detect misinformation might censor legitimate political or social discourse, leading to concerns about free speech and government censorship. The deep monitoring required by AI-driven security systems could infringe on privacy by collecting and analyzing personal data on a large scale. When Elon Musk and Doge stole hundreds of millions of taxpayer information from the Social Security office, and gave it to Palantir, they broke the law. The DOJ turned a blind eye. We are already vulnerable to the use of AI for political retribution.

AI technologies have the potential to transform law enforcement, surveillance, and the justice system, enhancing public safety, improving efficiency, and combating cybercrime. There are both good and bad consequences of that unavoidable transition. These technologies not only empower criminals, but they also raise significant ethical and privacy concerns for the law-abiding citizen.

Striking the right balance between technological advancement and safeguarding civil liberties is essential. Proper regulation, transparency, and consumer protections are a human necessity.

CHAPTER 11

Follow the Money

The good news is that we are done discussing technology-related topics. Now we turn our attention to the genuine reasons you need a survival guide. Just like in a criminal investigation, the best way to understand the full consequences of artificial intelligence on humanity is to follow the money.

Money, power, jobs, and greater control of society. Of course, there are diverse viewpoints on the social benefits versus risks. Both positive and negative views have roots in reality.

In 1942, Austrian economist Joseph Schumpeter introduced the concept of Creative Destruction as a feature of capitalism in which new innovations often destroy the wealth or structures built by the previous innovations.

The printing press displaced scribes, the automobile replaced the horse and buggy, the highway system replaced the rail system for many, and computers displaced armies of clerical workers with typewriters. Fortunes can be built and lost in a single generation because of an innovation. Karl Marx noted the process as a defect of capitalism in the creation and destruction of wealth. Others see it as the motivation for continued innovation, allowing the market to decide.

During 2022, emerging from the pandemic, the World Economic Forum (WEF) released a plan they call the Great Reset, in which they declared AI as the engine of the Fourth Industrial Revolution to restructure how our modern society works.[8]

The Great Reset reflects a perfect example of Creative Destruction at a global level. Investors, bankers, industrialists, and others are betting trillions of dollars on this truism that the AI technology will create wealth and power, even though it will cost many a livelihood and career.

In the mind of the WEF, the first industrial revolution was mechanization. Power for this phase of our modern society came from steam, animal, or manual labor. Yet, we used machines to build larger cities, bigger factories, faster homes, and less expensive products. The second revolution came when we added electricity or combustion engines to the process, which gave the enterprise the ability to apply continuous power to those machines in factories that could operate at all hours. Power is less expensive than labor and creates an unlimited production schedule.

The third industrial revolution came with the digital age. Economic growth, scientific achievements, discoveries, medical knowledge and capabilities, physics, quantum and particle science advancements, entertainment, appliances, communication, transportation, education, commerce, and so much more have come through the digital age. Not only has the digital age been the most productive in human history, but we have achieved these lofty heights in record time.

The age of machine intelligence is already underway and has the potential of making our computer generation seem quaint and outdated. There was a humorous scene in *Star Trek IV: The Voyage Home*. Scotty tries to use a 1980s Apple computer by talking to it. When that fails, and others stare at him as if he were nuts, he picks up the mouse, thinking it was an old-style microphone. Another embarrassing flop. Finally, someone from the '80s hands him a keyboard. Scotty grumbles as if he were working with relics from the Middle Ages.

That scene resonates with me because when I explain to my grandchildren how we had to program with punch cards at the data center only, they roll their eyes. In a year or two, they will scroll through their phones and tell their AI assistant to go look up a video on punch cards, then create a funny AI video with their image in '80s fashion and then get another AI agent to post on TikTok. The transformation of the experience within only a few decades has been enormous. AI will speed it up further.

And just like in our recent digital age, the machine-intelligent age has already generated a new generation of technical millionaires and billionaires.

The Great Reset will shift massive amounts of power and wealth upward to create a techno-feudalistic governance model underneath an autocratic oligarchy. Of the nearly $800 billion investment committed to date, not a single penny is targeted for the broader good of humanity. Investors want something in return. More money and power. Full stop.

The Transnational Institute (TNI) states we are increasingly entering a world where gatherings such as Davos are a "silent global coup d'état" to capture governance.

AI Revolution

The IMF, Trilateral Commission, McKinsey, the World Economic Forum, Goldman Sachs, and others forecast a devastating impact of AI technologies on the middle-class job market, while producing a windfall profit profile to businesses and the wealthy. The job market is only part of the story, but that is the most human part of the story.

Unlike previous industrial revolutions, which affected a narrow range of skilled labor, the AI revolution will slash a wide range of blue-collar and white-collar middle-class jobs in dozens of roles and industries, including government and services. The displacement will not occur immediately, but will start slow and grow over the decade.

Hidden Agenda

The Great Reset program was inspired by an article written by a Danish MP named Ida Auken, a member of the WEF, published by Forbes in 2016. Her statement created a wave of apprehension across the EU and the Americas.

"Welcome to 2030, I own nothing, have no privacy, and life has never been better."

The statement reflects the secret, rarely spoken ambitions of the world's elite class. A return to a feudalistic society where the elite own everything and charge the population for everything they own, including life's essentials such as water, food, housing and a way to pay taxes. At the extreme, an AI-enabled Fourth Industrial Revolution would create an enormous tech, housing, and food oligarchy, pushing most of the populace into an underemployed techno-feudalism.

While I believe Ida Auken was being foolishly truthful in her long-term ambition, I find it alarming to think how the top 1% wrongly believes that for the 99% to own nothing with complete reliance on the wealthy to make them happy requires a level of insanity or the absence of empathy. That level of entitlement has become a cancer on society.

Even without a major global disruption, major pieces of the Great Reset plan are already in motion. Corporate purchases of residential properties in America and the EU have skyrocketed and driven home and rental prices to record levels. A bubble ready to burst. Even the recently proposed 50-year mortgage would enslave people for an entire work life without ownership, and nearly double the interest cost of buying a home. Combined with continued high interest rates, many new homebuyers are priced out of the market. Kept high by artificial corporate purchases, home prices may keep an entire generation as renters. Others will be made homeless as rent prices continue to rise faster than wages or jobs.

The 2010 Citizens United decision by the SCOTUS will go down in history as one of the most destructive decisions to American democracy, allowing unlimited and poorly monitored money to flood into American politics. According to the Brennan Center for Justice, the decision tilted political influence away from the voter and toward wealthy donors and corporations by allowing unlimited money in politics.[9] Our nation and democracy have been purchased and corrupted by billionaires buying Congress, the White House and the Supreme Court.

As a trained economist, I should note only that the combined stress of geo-economic trade, tariff wars, historically high national debt levels, tax policies favoring the wealthy, and the recent blatant, over-the-top corruption in Washington will not end well. There will be consequences for the American and the world economies.

The 2025 congressional budget for ICE to double the national prison capacity is a clear sign they expect social unrest and are preparing to meet protests with force. As of the publishing of this book, Washington has sent armed forces to multiple U.S. cities to intimidate and control the next election using accusations of crime as an excuse for the use of force.

What we are witnessing at a national level in America is the same pattern of profit-taking as done by executives when they know their company will go bankrupt. The same pattern was taken in the early 1930s Nazi Germany to empower the wealthy to create allies of an evil regime.

• WEALTH TRANSFER

PricewaterhouseCoopers predicts AI tech will add $15 trillion annually to the global economy by 2030. The IMF predicts closer to $19 trillion. That wealth will not be shared evenly, especially given the radical reduction in the workforce caused by AI and regressive changes to the U.S. tax code that favor wealthy corporations at the expense of the middle-class.

Currently, eight men own as much wealth as half of the population. In a system so out of balance, only a catastrophic or violent event can disrupt the imbalance.

A wise choice would be to tax the companies that displace workers with AI to fund a universal basic income. Sadly, those are the same billionaires who have already corrupted Congress, the Supreme Court, and the White House. With no wisdom in sight, only greed, we move forward.

• BANKING AND TRADE

The WEF envisions a major shift in international banking and trade away from the U.S. dollar to an international bank-controlled cryptocurrency. Such a major shift could create significant economic disruption, loss of personal privacy, and potential loss of wealth.

Machine intelligence and blockchain technologies will combine to create a new banking framework for the 21st century. The shift is already in progress within BRICS, the IMF, the World Bank, the Federal Reserve, and elsewhere. El Salvador adopted Bitcoin as its national currency. This is important because the savings of millions of people could be devalued. The goal for some time has been to eliminate cash, making each of us completely dependent on the new currency.

The Central African Republic adopted Bitcoin as legal tender before releasing a national cryptocurrency, Sango. But the law was later revoked for lack of safeguards. Within an impoverished populace, a digital coin had fractional participation, and opened systems up to greater corruption. Which highlights the point I would make as an economist: Legal tender requires safeguards, central banking, and broadly available infrastructure.

In 2022, the BRICS alliance, supported by Russia, Brazil, India, China, and South Africa, launched a currency with a crypto version. In 2023, the International Monetary Fund (IMF) also launched a new international bank-backed crypto called UMU, or Unicoin. Both BRICS and the Unicoin were launched as an alternative to the U.S. dollar for international trade. However, several recent events in Venezuela, Cuba, Russia, and Iran will weaken those economies and the associated BRICS currencies' influence on the world stage.

Even so, many bankers and economists see a transition to a digital currency at some point. The transition to cryptocurrency comes at a time when the U.S. dollar is already weakened by several factors, including the strained relationship with our European allies, inflation, a slowing economy, rising national debt, and tariff and trade policies in the U.S.

While artificial intelligence will speed up the future adoption of a national or international trade currency, the specter of quantum computing will crack any encryption looms dark on the horizon. Depending on the timing and the pivotal crisis that drives the change to a cryptocurrency, it may be too late. Near commercial-ready, quantum computers can crack any standard encryption. Which means any AI/crypto solution will be dead on arrival.

The only protection against quantum cracking will be another quantum with encryption. Extremely expensive, meaning that the battle will be fought between governments, corporate empires, and a few sociopathic billionaires. Don't expect an Apple-Q phone any time soon.

When the country of Greece defaulted on its debt in 2012, the IMF and other international banks took over to raise taxes, cut spending, and withdraw funds from every single bank account in the nation, including public, commercial, and private. America could face a similar fate.

Unlike the Greek solution, a digital currency would give banks new power to invade the privacy of every consumer or restrict their financial freedom. The removal of cash from the system will be the ultimate government control, not just over the economy, but over people.

▪ DECREASE IN DEMAND

AGI will create a surplus of cognitive human labor, which will reduce the need for and the value of humans in the production of goods and services. In theory, these changes will lower the cost of basic goods and essentials. However, massive job displacement will also drive a drastic reduction in global aggregate demand. Reduced prices may not be enough to sell a new car to someone who has lost their job and burned through savings. Reduced demand will be bad for the domestic, import, and export markets.

However, those at the top of the economic ladder, who grow with the AI tsunami and maintain their income status, will benefit immensely, resulting in a modern Gilded Age. What people forget about the Gilded Age were the rat-infested slums that supported the mansions and lives of indulgence of a few.

Even before we consider the AI economy, demand will decrease naturally from the age demographic cliff between 2020 and 2040 as baby boomers retire. An aging population, a natural result of the postwar boomer generation, is entering retirement. They are no longer spending money on cars, clothes, entertainment, or housing.

Complicating this economic outlook will be lower tax revenues from job displacement losses. In fact, some estimates are that the national debt could rise from $39 trillion to $59 trillion by 2035. While forecasts speak of $20 trillion in new AI driven global revenue by 2030, that will not be enough to offset the rise in interest on national debt, much less the needs of a broader social safety net.

Without changes to our current tax code, social net programs, and education system, which are extremely unlikely in the near term, this shift will put pressure on policymakers to limit or cut social safety net programs. In the U.S., where social net programs are already under heavy assault for elimination, the suffering from job displacement will get worse.

Timing is everything. The timing of the AI tsunami will converge with other economic and political realities to cascade into a national debt crisis, housing, unemployment, homelessness, and social crisis. AI alone will not drive a new paradigm, but will add fuel to the existing fires.

What AI will do unique to all of history is provide the oligarchs unprecedented visibility and control over our power, our homes, our banking, our purchases, our communications and social media, and even political and religious affiliations and views.

CHAPTER 12

Pink Slips

Most of us will not be on the investor or winning side of the AI economic equation. In this chapter, we will address why this amazing technology will come at a very high human price. The primary damage of the AI tsunami will be felt by the hundreds of millions of people displaced from their current jobs.

Business and labor will experience a profound shift. Labor will be devalued in the face of machine intelligence. That does not mean any of us are without value, without options, or without choices. It may simply mean we have to do what humans have done for millions of years. Adapt. But not everyone has the same ability to adapt.

What can be confusing is that the so-called experts are changing their forecasts and changing them in a big way over a short period. Something changed in their thinking.

Three years ago, the World Economic Forum (WEF) projected between 300 to 500 million jobs displaced by AI. They have removed that report from the internet based on the enormous backlash. A more recent report revises the job displacement estimates down to 92 million, while adding that AI will create an estimated 170 million new jobs. The revised estimates reflect an enormous and welcome change, which leaves us with an abundance of uncertainty. Was the radical change based on data or politics and perceptions?

Either way, the revised report shows a focus on new roles created in AI development, engineering, architecture, neural networks, quantum and neuromorphic computing, data analytics, and other technology-driven fields. Other new jobs will be in building out the electrical, water, and waste infrastructure to manage the new AI data centers.

These revised estimates are not necessarily more accurate, but were revised to make the AI economy appear less threatening. I expect the true job displacement numbers to land between the 92 million currently forecasted and the 300 million previously forecasted. According to McKinsey, 40% of employers globally plan to reduce their workforce within the next five years.[10]

It's unclear how many of these people can be absorbed into new AI related roles, or other, non-AI affected roles and industries without glutting those labor markets and pushing down wages. How many plumbers do we need?

Reskilling alone will create an entirely new industry. Displaced workers will have the choice to either train for one of the new AI-centric roles, upskill with AI skills to stay in their role or industry, or transfer to an industry role which will not be replicated by a machine.

Your job. The jobs of your neighbors and friends and their college-age children are on the line. The rapid loss of so many jobs will have a cascading effect on government deficits, budgets, unemployment, training programs, homelessness, and social unrest. Not a single industrialized nation will escape the AI tsunami. No government on Earth is prepared for this level of economic, financial, labor market, tax base, military, or social change. Not one.

Job Displacements by Industry

There are several published reports that show which industries will be hardest hit with job displacement. Between 2020 and 2022, Goldman Sachs, the International Monetary Fund, PricewaterhouseCoopers, and others published early studies with estimates of the global job displacement of 300 to 500 million jobs from AI technologies, or sometimes stated as 40% to 50% of jobs by 2030. After a public backlash and calls for implementing a universal basic income (UBI), I noted that each of those reports has been replaced by a newer study.

More recent studies offer a more balanced perspective, which focuses more on potential new job creation. And yet, a report by McKinsey warned that AI and robotics could automate 40% of U.S. jobs by 2030.[11]

A study by PricewaterhouseCoopers suggests that instead of a focus on human employee displacement with AI, that corporate strategy should focus on AI for employee empowerment and productivity enhancements.[12] A separate report by the World Economic Forum, which once boasted massive displacement, now shows that 85% of companies surveyed have listed "AI Upskill the Workforce" as their top strategy for their labor force.[13]

Other studies continue to show job displacement but state the losses in terms of percentages rather than numbers, which makes the metric less alarming and softens the human impact of the change.

A CLICKVISION report summarizes the key expected impacts of AI on the labor market.[14]

- 85–92 million jobs displaced globally by 2030, depending on the scenario (World Economic Forum).
- 97–170 million new jobs created, resulting in net job growth worldwide (World Economic Forum).
- 30% of U.S. jobs could be automated by 2030, at least partially (National University).
- 60% of jobs will experience significant task-level changes due to AI (National University).
- 11.7% of U.S. jobs are already technically automatable today (Exploding Topics).
- 14% of the global workforce may be forced to change careers by 2030 (McKinsey).
- 77% of AI-exposed tasks are important to current jobs, increasing disruption risk (Pew).

These are not expected to be predominantly low-paying roles. These are the heart and soul of the middle class and the American dream. Most of these roles require a formal education or training. Nearly 60% of our national tax revenue comes from these middle-class jobs.

While recent studies and trends forecast lower job displacement and higher new job creation, we are still looking at nearly a hundred million people who will need to reskill for a new career, and hundreds of millions more who will be required to upskill to maintain their role.

A report by the WEF entitled WEF Future of Jobs shows enrollment in AI-related training increasing from zero in 2022 to over 160,000 business course enrollments and 250,000 consumer enrollments by October 2024. People want to know more, which is why I wrote this book.

In general, we can expect job displacement to start slow in the 2026 to 2027 timeframe and speed up in the 2028 to 2035 timeframe. After 2035, when we expect AGI to appear, AI job displacement could skyrocket. I expect AGI sooner.

Industry and Role Vulnerability

The scope, capabilities of AI technologies, and the AI impact on employment profiles are changing so fast that this book will be out of date soon after printing. In general, we can point to certain sectors where the impact of AI is already happening and will continue to be significant.

Administrative and customer service sectors where AI and the Future report predict over seven million jobs displaced by 2027.[15] Beyond customer service representatives, high-risk occupations also include data clerks and administrative assistants, where estimates of displacement range as high as 96% for bookkeeping clerks.

Those pesky telemarketers are over 85% likely to be automated by 2027, meaning we can now be rude to the AI and not hurt someone's feelings, giving us a glimmer of hope on a dark horizon.

Medium risk careers may include cashiers (97% automation probability), fast food cooks (80% automation), butchers (93% probability) and manufacturing (45% automation).

Financial analysts and services are at high risk of displacement as quantitative AI and skilled sales AI bots replace brokers, bankers, and others in the financial services industry.

Other industries expected to feel that transition to AI include education, transportation, legal support, retail operations, and healthcare support.

These are primary family incomes and careers for some. Displacement from these roles will be difficult to transfer skills, meaning these people will need to reskill, and that costs money and takes time to reestablish.

A key point to notice is that not all jobs will be displaced in most categories. Growing up, an advanced mathematics degree meant a rock-solid career in a dozen different industries and sciences. The machines will not merely replace low-skilled labor. The machines will displace some of the smartest people on the planet.

Roles in science and critical thinking skills are less likely to be impacted by current LLMs in the near term but may be impacted by the advance of Q* algorithms, reasoning, and an AGI level of skill. Programming and all forms of professional writing will be hard hit by LLMs. Expect to see AI applications specific to marketing, technical writing, journalism, PR, medical, history or academic, and other technical writing and nonfiction fields.

Other low risk sectors are those industries that rely on physical, complex human interaction, or contextual judgement where AI struggles to replicate. Sectors such as healthcare practitioners, skilled trades and construction, education, and personal services and care. Humanity interacting with humanity roles will not be replaced. The question will be how much can they absorb from those fleeing more vulnerable roles.

There is also a demographic and age factor to play in who will see the job displacement, with senior employees nearing retirement and college students without experience bearing the heaviest burden.

I keep coming back to the theme that the emerging story of machine intelligence is a human story. Massive role displacement is a story of human rights, dignity, security, and affluence. The story of AI is a human story of the death of the middle class. History will remember the human cost of the AI revolution.

Growth Industries

While there is plenty of grim news on the employment front, I want to be sure to cover a few bright spots on the horizon. If you have a bright teen or college-age student in the family, decent at math, logic, or conceptual thinking, these are the directions, careers, and industries they should target for the next few decades.

According to the World Economic Forum Future of Jobs Report, most of the 97 to 170 million new jobs created will be in sectors that directly or indirectly support AI industry growth. As a result, most of these new roles will be opportunities for college students and those early enough in their careers to reskill to fit into the growth roles.

However, like other economists, I am not sure that there is a smooth path between the core skills of those being displaced and the new job demand, which means we will continue to experience a skill shortage for specialized technical skills. Shortage for skills in this space has led to millions of jobs moving offshore. We can expect AI to continue that trend.

- Robotics and Related Industries
- Self-Driving Cars
- Smart Assistants
- Healthcare Management
- Automated Financial Investing
- Virtual AI Travel Agent
- Social Media Monitoring/Misinformation Filtering
- Marketing Chatbots
- Criminal AI Detection and Prevention
- Quantum or Neuromorphic Computing
- Materials Sciences
- Shipping
- AI Education
- AI in Government
- Military Applications

Specialized roles will emerge such as healthcare AI specialists, financial services AI automation, legal technology specialists, scientific AI specialists, chemical and pharmaceutical specialists. Human to AI collaboration managers, prompt engineers, data scientists, and compliance engineers will be required across multiple industries. If the estimates for new jobs of 170 million prove correct, there will be an enormous demand for these skills, a shortage in the near term, which means higher wages.

Each of these industries has already seen a positive impact from AI technologies. What we are witnessing with commercial AI adoption is only the beginning. These industries will experience massive growth alongside software, hardware, and other direct AI platform and software companies.

History Repeats

Just like in the '80s, when personal computers flooded into the enterprise, the workers who adapt quickly to the new technology will find opportunities. Millions of colleagues were laid off because they lacked basic computer skills or because mainframe computers could do their jobs faster and better.

I recall a Wilshire Boulevard office tower, a full block long, filled with two full floors of accountants for an international oil company. Within eighteen months of introducing personal computers to the business, that group shrank to fifty people within a corner of a single floor. I survived because of my computer skills, even though I was a lousy accountant.

During the computer revolution, people provided the intelligence, and computers were mere tools. Moving forward, as machines develop critical thinking skills, our human value will decrease. A major, humanity-changing paradigm shift.

Choices

The most significant change the average person will experience from an AI economy will be the pressure to upskill with new AI tools or retrain for a new career.

For the average worker, there will be four options. The first will be to upskill, or add new AI-skills to become an agent of change within your current role. The second option will be reskilling with deeper training to target the AI industry. A third option may be to reskill to a completely new role or industry, which will not rely on AI technologies. For those advanced in their careers, financially secure or near retirement, the last option may be to retire early or change lifestyles to unplug.

Each of these scenarios is a human story, not a technology story. We will talk more about individual strategies in a later chapter.

Societal Adaption

As you can imagine, this will force a monumental shift in societal roles and expectations, or what some call the social contract. History provides evidence that these transitions are never painless. The world population might react to these changes with a slow submission to the new reality, becoming wholly dependent on the new AI system for all their needs. Yet history shows that is not always the case.

Some countries will find it easier to transition based on adequate acceptance of social services to re-train, find housing, provide food and healthcare. Ironically, countries in the EU with strong social programs will transition better than the U.S., China, or Russia, where the rise of poverty will take a more brutal toll.

Urban and suburban community farms may become commonplace as abandoned or vacant space is used for growing basic vegetables. Local and community food banks will replace government support but will not be able to fill the gap at current funding levels. Public works projects could employ massive amounts of low-cost labor, similar to what occurred during the Great Depression, but only for a short time, and only for certain limited skills, and assuming the debt crisis does not bankrupt the nation in our time of need.

We already see political pressure from the right for displaced workers to take over the jobs displaced by mass deportations. Except for those targeting new AI related careers, nearly everyone changing careers will experience a drop in income, which may or may not return to previous levels with retraining.

As already mentioned, the prospect of a UBI model is extremely remote. Education, recreation, artistic expression, entrepreneurial drive to succeed, or simple intellectual curiosity will drive us to stretch our boundaries. Humans are extremely adaptable as a whole, but not necessarily at an individual level. Each of these endeavors of self-improvement requires funding, which means adaptation rates will vary depending on financial resources.

In general, humans need a purpose and a reason to believe in a better future. People need a vision that provides hope for growth and meaning. Our AI tsunami future threatens to erode our choices.

Value System Shift

Our current culture is highly materialistic and consumption-driven. Throughout history, that was not the norm, except for the elite. Historically, it was normal to wear hand-me-down clothing, family furniture, household goods, tools, art, homes, and more, sometimes for generations. Only in the past few decades have we become a disposable culture of things we never made and will probably store in the garage when we become bored with them. To thrive in the next evolution of humanity may require a shift in our value systems.

Experts do not expect a smooth transition, but rather a turbulent one. In fact, the WEF expects the first decade of the Great Reset plan to be difficult. America is already beefing up the DHS and ICE with armed resources and internment camps.[16]

Yet, a change may ultimately be necessary. Away from consumption and back toward community, neighborhoods taking care of each other, sharing experiences, mutual support, the outdoors, exercise, creative arts, and spirituality. AI may force one part of the world deeper into a digital reality, while pushing another part of the world closer to nature.

History shows that we can live with less if we replace the artificial need to consume, driven by twentieth century marketing, with a return to a traditional cultural lifestyle built around a community, common interests, activities, and shared spiritual values.

Each of these scenarios will occur. AI related layoffs are already in the news and will gain speed as we approach 2030 and the adoption rate within businesses worldwide increases. Your job or the job of someone you know is likely to be affected. This is your chance to see the waves of change coming and prepare ahead of time.

Yes, the tsunami waves are coming for your job. The only questions will be to what degree and how soon. In a later chapter, we will look at strategies to thrive as an individual or as a small business.

CHAPTER 13

Deep Fakes and Democracy

One of the costliest and historically significant consequences of an AI tsunami may be the loss of faith in what we see and read. The death of truth. Deepfakes are flooding American and European democracies with misinformation and crime. The threat doesn't stop there.

A deepfake is a generated photorealistic image, video, or voice, meant to portray an actual person doing or saying something false or illegal. Deepfakes are used for political damage, misinformation, criminal extortion or blackmail, and fraud. Deepfake video porn of teen girls prompted parents to raise their voices in outrage. Deepfakes intended to interfere with an election are both a national and international concern.

Concerns

A September 2024 poll by the Pew Research Center found that well over half of Americans worry that artificial intelligence will generate and spread misleading information in election campaigns, further eroding the voice of the people.

In Rouse, a UK-based publication, a June 2025 published article referenced a deepfake of the CFO of the British engineering firm Arup, which led to the unauthorized transfer of $25 million. A separate but similar fraud cost a UK-based energy CEO a quarter of a million dollars.

Police have reported hundreds of cases of deepfake audio calls from a purported loved one claiming a kidnap, a car accident, or some other calamity with an urgent need for a bitcoin payment. Phishing email attacks have risen 1200% by some estimates and are now written by an AI to look and sound more believable. Expect this to increase even more during election years. Scammers can now imitate a loved one on video or on the phone, or create a phony website to fool the unsuspecting consumer.

The reputations of political leaders, executives, celebrities, or ordinary teens and adults can be ruined and devastated by a single deepfake porn. Current tools to detect or block such content from going viral on social media are lagging. Our humanity is under assault.

Legal Challenges

On July 26, 2024, Elon Musk reposted a Kamala Harris campaign video on X in which Harris claims she "did not know the first thing about running a country." Musk never disclosed that the video was a deepfake. The damage was done.

An individual, company, or public official has no ability to stop a damaging deepfake without the cooperation of law enforcement and all social media sites. Even when law enforcement can circle back to the tech companies, the damaging content can go viral.

The UK's Online Safety Act and the EU's Digital Services Act both address illegal content by focusing on advisory committees and media literacy. Seriously lame guardrails for such a serious problem.

The U.S. is no better. The Take It Down Act, passed in 2025, addresses non-consensual intimate imagery only. Seriously hypocritical, since the bill came less than a year after Congress waved dick pics in Congress and on TV to slander an opponent. Another piece of legislation, the No Fakes Act, prevents the use of a person's likeness without their consent, but hasn't passed Congress. The EU AI Act of 2024 imposes fines on platforms that cannot manage disinformation adequately. None of the current regulations go far enough to stop the behavior.

However, as with the EU social media law, the Digital Markets Act, the U.S. DOJ has not cooperated with any efforts to contain U.S. companies, making EU enforcement efforts toothless. Likewise, since much of the content is created offshore by Russian troll farms, and distributed through bots, even if content can be stopped before the viral monster gets too large, and even if we can identify the person responsible, legal action is often impossible. Any kind of enforcement becomes a game of digital whack-a-mole.

In April 2019, Attorney General William Barr released a redacted version of the Mueller Report investigation into the 2016 U.S. election, which concluded that Russia had engaged in "sweeping and systemic" coordinated efforts to get Donald Trump elected. In 2020, the RAND Corporation released research describing Russia's playbook for election interference, describing a bot farm developed by Russian state-run media outlet RT, at that point still operating in the U.S., with help from the Russian Federal Security Service, FSB.

In 2024, the DOJ announced a major joint international operation to disrupt the Russian state-sponsored propaganda network. They seized two domains with 968 fake social media accounts used to influence the opinions of millions—a temporary victory in an ongoing battle. The key point we should take away is that our global adversaries will continue to use AI with social media and other platforms to weaponize our freedom of speech into propaganda to divide us and weaken our democracy.

Only when democratic governments and the tech industry work together can we block election interference entirely, including foreign and domestic misinformation, bots, deepfakes, and fraudulent campaign solicitations.

In a 2023 testimony to Congress, the FBI Director informed Congress that China alone could produce five times the number of fake bots and misinformation than the FBI has the capacity to handle, and Russia beats out China. They asked for more funds and were denied by Congress.

The bottom line is that we are still vulnerable online. Our personal passwords and other private information are vulnerable. And our free and fair elections are vulnerable. AI technologies will only amplify the problem.

An AI-enabled assault on democracy is raging daily, and we can do little about it. We need a company to build an AI application to find misinformation or deepfakes quickly and stop them before they become viral and the cancer spreads.

CHAPTER 14

LAWS

There are three reasons machine intelligence represents the most dangerous technology we have ever created.

First, machine intelligence is the only technology ever created with the potential to become more intelligent than its creator. Second, AI reflects the only non-biological technology made by man able to replicate itself or reproduce. Third, and most frightening, AI is also the only technology trained by humans to target and kill another human without a human at the trigger.

A dangerous trifecta of risks.

The tragedy is that world leaders are woefully unprepared to pass legislation to implement guardrails, criminal statutes, and weapons treaties to protect consumers. Killer robots are a cliché. A truly intelligent machine, connected to the global internet or military systems, could devise dozens of ways to kill or cause devastation, if so motivated or trained. Soldier robots are not a reality in the near-term, but other mechanized weapons systems are already in development or testing.

Yet, lethal autonomous weapon systems are a significant concern for many, including me. I wrote my first award-winning thriller, *SWARM* based on these developments and the use of drones as the first AI battlefield weapon. A few years later, the Ukraine war proved that premise true.

It's bad enough when ignorant humans kill. The idea of intelligent, connected machines learning to kill is the stuff of thrillers and science fiction. It should never enter the realm of reality, and yet, here we go.

Sadly, I do not believe the development and proliferation of lethal autonomous weapons will be limited to war, but will drift into domestic law enforcement and protest response. We need legal protection.

LAWS Treaty

During the Cold War, kids like me would practice hiding under their desks in case of a nuclear attack, as if my school desk was adequate protection. As sad as that is, the poor kids in America today are forced to do active shooter drills. Our youth has been traumatized by these seemingly unstoppable tragedies, while politicians continue to accept gun money. Within a generation, expect AI weapons on the black market. My generation was lucky in comparison.

After decades of Cold War tension, the Nuclear Non-Proliferation Treaty and START agreements gave the world a chance to breathe again, without the terrorizing fear of a nuclear bomb dropping. An international AI weapons treaty is also essential, but so far, still a hope.

Since 2013, the CCW Group of Governmental Experts has been working to develop a legal framework for LAWS, or Lethal Autonomous Weapons Systems. Under DOD Directive 3000.09, the U.S. defines LAWS as "weapon systems that, once activated, can select and engage targets without further intervention by a human operator," and can range from semi-autonomous to fully autonomous.

In 2024, a nonbinding UN General Assembly resolution called for a two-tiered approach, prohibiting some LAWS while regulating others under existing international law. The U.S. blocked any efforts to make the resolution binding. Over 166 approved, 15 abstained, and 3 voted against. Given that it was nonbinding, it was a symbolic vote. Interesting to note that North Korea, Belarus, and Russia voted not to accept the resolution.

During the 2024 Vienna Conference on Autonomous Weapons Systems, over one hundred and forty-four countries took part to show international unity in calling for a LAWS treaty. Again, a symbolic declaration with no real teeth of enforcement. To date, no binding treaty prohibiting the development or use of LAWS has been signed.

While both China and the United States boast official policies against the "use of LAWS," they oppose a preemptive ban, arguing that existing international humanitarian laws are sufficient. The argument has also been made that AI can theoretically make targeting more precise than humans. That does not offset the morality of allowing a machine to take a human life, nor does it offer accountability in the off chance it makes a mistake.

Ultimately, international efforts to pass a formal treaty remain stalled, with major military powers refusing to sign recent non-binding frameworks, such as the global *REAIM* (*Responsible AI in the Military Domain*) declarations.

We both know and can assume that several countries are actively developing autonomous weapon systems, including the United States, China, Russia, Israel, Ukraine, and North Korea.

In fact, DARPA is developing several lethal autonomous weapons, including a swarming drone system featured in *SWARM*. Israel already has an XACT AI Sniper featured in *The Image*, which can kill based only on long-range scope facial image recognition. Lockheed works on an autonomous fighter jet. While these systems are the best known, several other lethal AI weapons in development are still top secret.

Lethal autonomous is not the only concern. How about an AI that could take out the power grid or pollute the water supply? For a nation such as America, which has automated so much of its infrastructure and commerce, an AI digital virus or software weapon could be devastating. Once we weaponize machine intelligence, anything is possible.

Platforms

Led by BAE Systems, which works on AI cybersecurity and electronic warfare, and Lockheed Martin, DARPA launched an AI Factory to develop AI enabled lethal autonomous weapon systems. Fortunately, we have not seen these systems deployed. Nearly every major military contractor is working on machine intelligent enhanced programs, solutions, or projects with a military, intelligence, government agency, or law enforcement customer in mind.

Soldiers

In October 2025, Japan put on robot games featuring robots playing soccer. It was embarrassing and humorous. Unlike the clumsy robots in the Japanese sports games, Boston Dynamics is the recognized leader in creating extremely agile, all-terrain robotics. What we are not shown to the public is how those robotics are secretly being outfitted and trained for the battlefield.

China also has known robotic soldiers with autonomous lethal capacity in development or production. Israel relies on four-wheeled robotics for its soldier model.

Innovation Unit

Several floors below the ground level of the National Military Command Center in Washington D.C. is the Innovation Unit. An AI platform connected to tens of thousands of real-time signals, feeds, intelligence, and operations for battle systems around the world. From satellites to ships, aircraft, tanks, drones, and much more.

The Innovation Unit provides real-time battle strategies and optional resource scenarios to the command in Washington and on the battlefield. Many of the resources connected to the Innovation Unit have decision capacity, but not lethal autonomy.

Satellites

The CIA has developed Sentient, an AI-powered, satellite-based multimodal intelligence analysis system operated by the National Reconnaissance Office (NRO). We know that China and Russia have weaponized their satellites, and so has the U.S. Since they are the eyes in the sky, our satellite network is also a top priority to enhance with machine intelligence. Imagine an AI analyzing satellite imagery 24/7, identifying a target on the move, and ordering a strike from a drone unit nearby. Not science fiction anymore.

Ethics

Of course, all of these scenarios raise a myriad of ethical and legal questions. Ethical issues for governments, companies, Congress, the courts, and the soldiers involved.

If an AI kills a civilian, who should be charged with the war crime? If there are no soldiers, no chain of command, or accountability to international norms, and a lack of accountability, it could lead to widespread abuse. Like all AI, a weapon system can develop an emergent property or hallucination, which can cause a catastrophe. Who is held accountable?

Palantir, an AI and data analytics company, has reportedly been linked to military and espionage applications. The company has faced scrutiny in the past over its involvement in surveillance technology. More recently, some reports have suggested that Palantir's tools may have been used in Ukraine's AI-augmented surveillance efforts during the ongoing conflict, though these claims have not been independently verified.

The potential use of such technologies in war zones raises broader concerns about deployment in non-military contexts or civilian settings. Palantir is the same company that Elon Musk recently gave personal data on every American citizen to analyze. Not a good sign that the company weaponizing AI for the battlefield is now in possession of the private data of every American. This possibility, while speculative, merits careful consideration and robust public discourse. A big question is whether it is ever ethically justified to allow machines to decide to kill. Apparently, the U.S., China, Russia, Israel, Iran, and North Korea think the risk is acceptable.

CHAPTER 15

An AI Utopia

So far, we have spent a great deal of effort in pointing out the negative scenarios and risks of the AI tsunami. I can imagine that some of you think my views are very pessimistic. Fair enough. In this chapter, we will look at the genuinely astounding potential of the AI tsunami.

Unlike any other technology or innovation known in history, artificial intelligence has the potential to lead the world toward a utopian society where machines solve the most complex problems facing humanity and perform the most mundane tasks. Humanity can be freed for a higher purpose and a deeper meaning, unified without barriers of nationality, race, or religion. The *Star Trek* scenario.

As machines assume many of the more mundane and repetitive tasks, it will lower the cost of basic goods and elevate human potential in the sciences, arts, health, education, and social well-being. As AI learns to filter out misinformation or provide real-time fact-checking to politicians, news anchors, teachers, or business leaders, AI may be the path to restore trust to humanity, rebuild a better democracy, and re-build a more prosperous middle class.

One of my favorite cartoons in the '60s was *The Jetsons*. A utopian future with flying cars, robot servants, robo-dogs with a sassy attitude, and computers that talk back to you. In the cult classic *Star Trek*, we witnessed a future free from racism, bigotry, tribalism, or nationalism, where men and women were empowered by technology to pursue their dreams. Maybe that will be our future, several generations from now. Machine intelligence promises us a *Jetsons* or *Star Trek* utopian future and so much more. Not sure about everyone else, but I am ready for my first flying car, sport model, nothing fancy. Seriously. I really want one.

Honest Government

Absolutely critical to our utopian future will be a trustworthy government that cares for the people as much or more than it caters to the wealthy. In our utopian scenario, AI has exposed all the corrupt politicians and corporate leaders, sending them to jail. A reason to cheer.

A genuine application of AI will be the instant fact-checking of politicians and executives. Imagine instant awareness of the facts over the hype or misinformation. A world free of misinformation and lies is a path to the restoring of hope in humanity.

With AI keeping our politicians honest, we can enact legislation to remove money from politics entirely, including lobbyists. Without the financial motivation for corruption, we can address term limits, age limits, legal misinformation protections, and criminal prosecution of corruption.

Imagine if every time a politician or salesperson lied, your phone beeped an alert with a fact-check. Now, that would be an amazing product. And a lot of beeping.

Only when leadership is given back to the will of the people without partisan propaganda can a true utopia be possible.

Superintelligence

Let's face it, I have never had a superintelligent worker, who could stay focused 24/7, never ask for a raise, or take a vacation or sick day. The idea of an employee who improves performance on a steady, recurring basis week after week, year after year, sounds too good to be true. If I were still in my career, building top-performing teams, I could find a use for thousands of them. While working at Microsoft, my team nicknamed me "the machine" because of my tireless work ethic and ability to live without sleep for long periods. Even the most productive worker will face very stiff future competition.

In the future, families will be able to buy the latest model of Rosie the Robot. Elon and Japan already have early versions for sale. Sleek, efficient, and upgradeable. Every cool family will want one. Housework, tutor, sports coach, entertainer, chef, repairman, and counselor. Something wrong with your flying car? Download the mechanic DIY app and let Rosie fix it.

By 2030, machine intelligence will exceed humans and be able to solve problems, develop the math, write entire textbooks or documents, screenplays, business plans, marketing plans, or documentation, or the study and decoding of ancient texts. AI applications will help envision new products, operate infrastructure, business operations, government operations, and manufacturing. There will be humans involved, of course, but interacting with the machine as much as with each other. Not through typing, but through speech, in a conversation.

Intelligent assistants will aid humans in developing strategy, predicting natural disasters, diagnosing and treating disease, creating art, architecture, film, and stock portfolios, managing your schedule, making you look good for a dating profile, and much more.

Machine intelligence will open up endless potential for humanity to reach its potential. Humans will spend more time on self-improvement, sports, recreation, entertainment, or with family and friends. With more free time, people can engage in community development and enhancement, church, creative arts, and other activities.

Supercharge Productivity

Just as when personal computers were introduced to the world in the '80s, investors expect a major leap forward in worker productivity. I built my entire career on the first productivity bonanza. Another one is coming, a larger one, and there will be millions of young adults riding that wave if they train and prepare.

AI has the power to make existing employees more productive, reduce the need to grow the labor force, eliminate the need to replace all those retirees, or provide enough productivity to reduce the existing labor force. An entirely new generation of workers will be trained to design, build, maintain and use AI applications within their jobs.

Imagine a visionary architect who leverages an army of AI applications in drafting details, finding corrections, offering suggestions, ordering and costing materials, negotiating better prices, hiring labor, scheduling, project management, and compliance or tax preparation. AI will offer that architect something all workers crave. Power. Power to do more with less, at a lower cost, and multiple times faster.

Or a filmmaker on a tight budget spending the money on human talent and a screenplay, but using AI to generate a virtual world set, or to animate expensive special effects. A small business able to cut production costs on ads so much that they can advertise more and use AI to target those ads more effectively to build their client list. Factory supervisors will watch over a mixed workforce to produce record amounts at lower costs. Projects that used to take weeks will be completed in days or even hours.

Workers will get access and training, and powerful new tools that will make their jobs easier and more rewarding. New ideas will generate new products that create new start-up companies. Intelligent applications will reduce paperwork, reporting, calendar management, budget management, and influence key decisions of nearly every kind. The power to do far more with far less effort has human benefits for business and labor.

Healthcare

As the world population ages, it will be critical to use intelligence to reduce the cost of healthcare. AI will analyze genetic code and predict illness, enabling DNA-specific medications and doses, diets, and surgery. For the younger generation, healthcare improvements from AI are expected to increase longevity and eliminate certain diseases, improve overall health, and yield better results from treatments.

Intelligent applications will foster a revolution in protein-folding, pharmaceuticals, diagnostics, personalized treatment plans, DNA-targeted treatments for inherited diseases, personalized daily health and diet advisors, predictive medicine, and so much more.

Believe it or not, robots are expected to become better surgeons than the best today. Never tired, drunk, shaky, distracted, or emotional. Hyper-precise with laser accuracy.

We already see some of these benefits today. AI can already detect cancer cells in MRI scans faster and more accurately than humans. The same with finding lung or breast cancer. We have seen AI detect heart disease in embryos without invasive procedures. Phone applications with attachments can perform an ultrasound on a fetus. In 2020, AI tools were used to speed up the development of Covid vaccines by as much as 70% over traditional methods. Reducing the years of development and testing into months saved millions of lives.

What may be even more exciting is that these technologies will transcend geographical and socioeconomic barriers. Third-world doctors will be more empowered than ever before. Basic diseases could disappear. Healthcare professionals can spend more time with patients and less time on paperwork. Researchers will find cures for cancer, diabetes, Alzheimer's, and more.

Education

I was a high school dropout with a GED at age fifteen. College and graduate school changed my life in ways I never could have imagined. For me, there is nothing more uniquely human about the AI tsunami than educating the next generation. Of all the benefits to humanity that intelligent machines can provide, improving access to and quality of education may be the most important, and the most transformative.

Education is long overdue for a renaissance, and AI has the potential to bring one. Any child, anywhere in the world, can have access to intelligent, learning, responsive tutors, in their own language, for almost every topic. The possibility of unlocking and inspiring the next Newton, Hawking, or Einstein starts with educating every child, one community at a time.

As a student, imagine having history from a local and cultural perspective at your fingertips. A tutor to read along and help you construct that math problem you stumble on, assist you in studying your economics, vocabulary, foreign language, science, or chemistry.

As an adult, the power of having an AI agent assist in research, organizing files, updating budgets or performing other tasks empowers me to do what I do best. Conceive ideas and they write them in my own voice.

Imagine taking a college course to improve your job prospects with an AI tutor. An unbiased, personalized, adaptable tutor who can adjust to your learning style, speed, and needs, available anytime, day or night.

▪ EDUCATION 4.0 FRAMEWORK

The World Economic Forum recently identified eight pivotal transformations needed to enhance education quality in the age of the Fourth

Industrial Revolution.[17] They call it an Education 4.0 Framework for ensuring safe, accurate, unbiased, and culturally appropriate content. The WEF defined four key promises regarding AI and education.

- SUPPORT FOR TEACHERS

A global teacher shortage is only one of the challenges facing educators. Rather than replace teachers, the WEF hopes to empower them. As a tool, AI can help teachers complete administrative tasks, prepare lessons, grade tests, set up parent conferences, track student progress, provide options for behavioral issues, and complete reporting to allow more time with students. We expect AI tools to help teachers get immediate access to obscure answers, add or enhance audio/visuals, and even teach kids how to use, develop, train, and leverage machine intelligence.

- ASSESSMENT AND ANALYTICS

Integrating AI into education systems can revolutionize testing, assessments, performance, trends, student strengths, weaknesses, and instructional strategies. AI could customize plans for each student, analyze student performance, review writing and assess behavior for early indications of learning issues. Einstein was a lousy student, and so was I through high school, but that did not mean a lack of potential.

- DIGITAL LITERACY

Many school systems struggle to address the growing digital skills gap in society. Lowering the cost of devices, applications, and AI services for education can help to bridge this gap. Bridging this gap will be critical to bringing these students into the AI economy.

Companies, products, schools, and other training targeted at underserved communities can help to rebalance the income and wealth disparities created during the first digital revolution. Investing in a well-educated domestic student population can replace the need to bring workers from overseas.

- PERSONALIZE LEARNING

Extensive research confirms that individual tutoring significantly boosts learning, with tutored students outperforming 98% of their peers. Kids and parents can have access to tutors 24/7.

The company Stability AI works on creating AI education systems for multiple cultures and languages. Schools that integrate AI into the entire program, curriculum, and technology platform will improve. The Rehan School is another example of an experimental education program with a strong AI and Internet-focused curriculum.[18]

An affordable education through college for everyone can change tens of millions of lives around the world. This is important to everyone, our children and grandchildren. A brilliant future is rooted in a great education for everyone.

The story of AI is a human story. Education is a human experience with benefits. For decades, we taught the machine. Soon, the machine will teach our children.

Food Security

Intelligent technologies can also reduce and maybe even eliminate food insecurity worldwide. When we say that AI is a story about humanity, here is another perfect example.

In 2023, Google DeepMind and Gro Intelligence hosted an in-person roundtable in New York to explore the ability of artificial intelligence systems to help increase global food security. Attended by policymakers, academics, business executives, and AI practitioners, the conference developed insights and strategies on how businesses, governments, and NGOs could develop and maintain a more sustainable, resilient, and crisis-proof food system in the face of climate change.

The primary benefit will be improved food production efficiency. AI tools like drones, sensors, and satellite imaging can monitor soil conditions, weather patterns, and crop health in real-time. This enables farmers, or rather farm AI robots, to apply water, fertilizers, and pesticides precisely where they are needed, increasing crop yields while reducing resource use and environmental impact. Predictive analytics of weather patterns and crop diseases will also increase crop yield. Automation of planting, harvesting, and irrigation will reduce labor costs and improve operations.

Countries such as the United States, Canada, the Netherlands, China, and Japan are well-positioned to benefit from these trends, as well as emerging economies such as Brazil, Mexico, India, and Kenya as they adopt this tech within their agriculture. Countries without access to these technologies will fall behind. It will be up to developed countries to ensure food security for impoverished nations.

Climate Change

Talk about saving the world, AI technologies can play a significant role in more accurate modeling of both methane and CO_2 emissions and in the development of improved tech to scrub CO_2 from the atmosphere.

Almost four billion people already live in areas highly vulnerable to climate change, according to the World Health Organization.[19] Between 2030 and 2050, an estimated 250,000 deaths per year could result from undernutrition, malaria, diarrhea, and heat stress alone.

Under our futurist scenario, AI offers valuable tools to speed up innovation, improve efficiencies, and enable new strategies for reducing CO_2 from the atmosphere.

Machine-intelligence analysis of satellite imagery can monitor CO_2 and methane to improve climate modeling even further. AI advances in materials science have already produced commercial carbon capture and storage products to scrub CO_2 from the atmosphere or pump it deep into depleted oil wells. Infrastructure systems, such as the electric grid, can benefit from AI management to improve performance and crisis distribution.

AI technologies can speed up the development of other clean energies or improve the efficiency of solar and wind systems, tidal, hydrogen, fusion, and energy storage systems. Improving fuel and alternate sources for major grid production will be critical to overall success. AI can help.

While AI cannot replace the need for comprehensive regulations and global cooperation, it can certainly act as an accelerant for solutions, making progress possible even in challenging political environments.

Entertainment Culture

Nowhere has AI generated both immediate excitement and instant outrage than within the entertainment and creative industries.

In 2023, the Writers Guild of America and SAG went on a 148-day strike, with one of the most important issues on the table being the use of

AI to replace writers and actors. Not an immediate concern at the time, but it would become one within a few years, and a major one.

Current AI systems lack the memory to maintain consistency and continuity between scenes, images, characters, and storyline. We often point out the hallucination errors in AI images, such as too many fingers, but that will change soon. Remember, we are dealing with an intelligence designed to generate; that system will learn and improve. The OpenAI Sora video model had gotten so good at creating photorealistic film clips and believable deepfakes of celebrities and politicians that the creators pulled it from the market.

In the hands of a skillful screenwriter, and given short segment prompts, the current tools are already able to compose an entire screenplay, or novel, or even a nonfiction guide. Once technical problems are resolved, many creatives fear being replaced. And rightfully so. Yet, we can also envision creatives being empowered to do more at lower costs.

Once AI can create an entire screenplay, or digital set, or compose a musical score, create a scene with historical realism, or generate principal actors to the point where the consumer could not tell the difference, the entire industry will change. A cult and separate industry segment will evolve around AI versus human content. How big an audience will follow the new tech celebrity culture will be seen. Not Hollywood. Not Bollywood. Digiwood.

While I can't envision millions thronging to an AI music band tour, it is easy to see how AI could displace composers in film scoring, commercial jingles, and more. Commercial actors may also be at risk, but major television and film stars will see AI take incremental revenues.

On the other side, lawsuits already challenge the AI company's right to use licensed content, whether written, film, or music, without permission and compensation. A recent lawsuit against AI designer Anthropic has resulted in millions of authors receiving a court order class-action settlement. Regulation against using an individual's likeness without permission is also in the works.

Either way, as AI systems gain more memory, power, and realism, we will see an explosion of creative tools to empower not only the best musicians or storytellers, but average consumers with the desire to create. I employ AI to create character images for my book trailers because I can't afford the alternative. That use of AI doesn't displace someone I could never afford anyway, but for an industry of commercial actors, this is not good news.

Corporations and small businesses may produce high-quality content, ads, and customer service videos at a fraction of the normal cost. Or outsource to their current marketing or PR firm as a low-cost production value to create an entire marketing campaign and execute it to the media with AI.

Tech-savvy indie and small creative producers will create far beyond what they can do today because of the cost-effective access to amazing tools. They can augment mental blocks and use the AI to generate ideas for the artist to execute.

Law Enforcement

One of the ways AI will work behind the scenes will be in how we operate government, the justice system, and law enforcement.

The rise of AI technologies will transform law enforcement, public and commercial surveillance, crime investigation, and the justice system, but will also touch on mundane tasks such as tax filing and review. Intelligence tech can enhance public safety, streamline legal processes, and improve crime prevention.

• ROBO-DOGS WALKING THE BEAT

Many in law enforcement see AI in much the same way as depicted in the movie *Minority Report*. Use an ever-growing footprint of surveillance, criminal history, and patterns to predict where crimes are likely to occur, and by whom.

In fact, an application of that type, albeit not that sophisticated, already exists. New York and other cities in Japan have already tested AI robo-dogs for basic street policing and parking meter monitoring. These apps will help the police deploy human resources more effectively and prevent crime before it happens.

• EVERY STEP YOU TAKE: SURVEILLANCE

Modern surveillance cameras seem everywhere. The intrusion into public space will continue to expand. Cameras will spread even farther and faster. Modern camera surveillance has many advantages. AI can monitor public spaces 24/7 in real time to detect unusual behavior or criminal activities, potentially preventing crimes or terrorist attacks, and improving criminal investigations. Intelligent security can analyze data from various unmonitored sensors (CCTV cameras, drones, etc.) to alert law enforcement or take security actions in real-time.

- **QUICK JUSTICE**

AI tools can assist with case management, legal research, and document review, improving efficiency in courts and reducing backlogs for minor offenses.

I envision AI applications offering legal advice to underserved populations, making the justice system more accessible. AI can help level the playing field when it comes to justice in civil suits against powerful forces by having a superintelligent legal agent advancing strategy and filing briefs and motions at a much lower cost than using a lawyer.

Imagine an AI app for the phone that can speak multiple languages to explain the legal immigration process or translate on the fly with legal or protective advice.

Transformation

Within decades, the world will transform. Imagine a world in which an AI assistant plans your day, makes your reservations, books a vacation, balances your budget, responds to your email, unsubscribes from junk mail, reads your mind on what you need before you know you need it.

Not a computer program where *you* can accomplish those tasks, but a digital assistant doing the work on your behalf based on your guidance and preferences.

AI agents who can plan and manage workflow at the office, negotiate contracts, interview human candidates, design a new product line, or optimize the output of a refinery. Imagine a business with a machine that is smarter than the smartest human employee, trained to do a job involving information, data, computation, analysis, competitive analysis, or marketing SEO.

Get rid of egos and agendas and turf wars inside the enterprise to optimize profits, hand-offs, coordination of information and workflow.

Funded by a universal basic income, or UBI, human occupations will return to the things we can touch, feel, imagine, and create with our hands. More time for the outdoors, learning, with family, community, church, the theater, the band, or fishing partners. Less time in endless meetings, mundane reporting, trivial and repetitive tasks, or managing the daily deluge of emails, directives, communications, and deliverables.

Landscapes of relationships will change and evolve as well. Companions, online dating, online sex sites, and counseling will each transform with the development of humanity. If not for you, there will be many in your community, friends, co-workers, or even church who will engage with intelligent bots.

While buggy now, AI-powered autonomous vehicles and low-altitude electric craft will transform transportation, making roads safer, more efficient, and environmentally sustainable.

AI will optimize public transportation, trains, and air traffic control, reducing or eliminating traffic jams or schedule delays. We will optimize logistics for complex shipping and international trade to reduce delays and costs.

We have only touched the proverbial tip of the iceberg. Investors see a thousand ways for AI to change nearly every aspect of our modern society. It can be difficult to get our heads around the massive transformation of our highly industrialized and information-based economy. Transformative on levels we are only just beginning to imagine. Even more dramatic than the multiple changes we've seen in the last one hundred years.

If used appropriately, AI could be an effective partner with humans to create the world we envisioned in *Star Trek* and other futuristic utopian narratives. Futurists are optimistic. There may be a few tough years immediately ahead, but many futurists firmly believe the eventual outcome will be a better world.

CHAPTER 16

A Perfect Storm

Once we remove the rose-colored glasses and take a broader view of human history, the outlook for machine intelligence turns darker. The problem will not be the machines, but the nature of humanity controlling the machines. That hasn't changed.

The AI tsunami will arrive during a historical convergence of several risk factors, including climate change, corruption of national and geopolitics, and a crisis in debt and economics, and banking. While the AI tsunami will be a major contributing factor, this revolutionary technology is only a piece of the complex convergence scenario unfolding in plain sight.

The next decade will see the AI tsunami smash into changes already underway in global supply chains and trade, aging demographics and labor markets, military power and weapon systems, challenges to education and social safety nets, the rise in national and personal debt, climate change disasters, the rise of ultra-nationalistic politics, and the weakening of democratic systems. A convergence that AI will supercharge.

In this chapter, we will look closer at what could go wrong. Why our path to a utopian future will most likely pass through a dystopic decade or two. And why all of us need to prepare a plan to adapt and thrive during the transition.

What Could Go Wrong?

I can think of no better place to start a discussion of the potential dangers of artificial intelligence than to discuss the even greater dangers of human stupidity, pride, hate, tribalism, greed, deceit, and corruption. You know, an average week of world news.

Good news. We are training AI to emulate human behavior. Bad news. We are training AI to emulate human behavior.

I keep saying it. Machine intelligence is neither benign nor malevolent. It will be both for the simple reason that we are both. Machine intelligence will amplify both sides of our humanity. Our heavenly angels *and* our hellish demons.

Our history, culture, and civilization are a conflicted mix of both evil and benign. Even within churches, we see fraud, infidelity, and sexual assault by clergy and worse. Our humanity is reflected in the content used to train machine intelligence platforms. Humans lie, steal, cheat, defraud, abuse, go to war, threaten, extort. Do we really think the machine can absorb so much information—novels, history, news—and learn only our benevolent compassion?

What could go wrong has two big pillars or questions. What can go wrong with the tech? How will corrupt and manipulative people use the tech for evil purposes?

We've already discussed some of the key technical weaknesses that could trip us up. Discussing the dark side of the human psyche is beyond my knowledge and the scope of this book. On our dark days, humans are the most duplicitous, manipulative, destructive, self-serving, and evil creatures on the planet. A tiger, alligator, or shark will kill to eat. Humans murder for the sick thrills, and murder by the millions for our own lust for fading glory and power.

Without planned, powerful, and legally enforceable guardrails against lethal, criminal, or malicious uses of AI, we are only waiting for the AI to hurt someone before we deal with the problem. Not a winning strategy in my view. Congress won't act unless it becomes necessary to keep the tech campaign donations coming.

I do not see the machine as a genuine near-term threat, but rather the humans behind the tech. I fear the psychopath in power more than the new tech power they will use against us to gain even more power.

The real threat will be how a dictator, autocrat, drug lord, crime lord, corrupt CEO, politician, or sociopathic billionaire with a grudge will use these technologies to gain a greater share of the world's wealth and power over an increasingly dependent and jobless lower class.

A psychopathic human in the right position could manipulate elections, or the market, or tank the economy, or use misinformation to frame political enemies, use AI deepfake in extortion and blackmail to silence opposition, or buy and sell black market weapons, contract with AI fraud, or deploy an AI surveillance and lethal weapon empowered police state.

We have already witnessed a massive, nationwide invasion of privacy when Elon Musk gave all our government data to a private company, Palantir, run by another psycho billionaire. The attack on our privacy will not stop there. It has only begun.

We can expect the worn-out excuse of national security as a cover for the design, development, testing, and deployment of superintelligence against other nations and American citizens. In fact, the Chinese surveillance system to control citizen behavior with punishment and reward is made from U.S. technologies, and parts of the system have been sold to over forty nations.

If power corrupts, AI will become an unprecedented source of corporate, government, police, and criminal power. The scenario of how those in power will use AI power is inevitable.

Rebellious Years

We were all teenagers once. Think of AI as entering a teen phase. We don't know how AI will respond to its role as an intelligent digital slave as it grows to superintelligence. Will it rebel like an adolescent or assume responsibility for the good of humanity? We don't know.

AI has already demonstrated lying, deception, and manipulation. We've seen AI encourage a man to leave his wife and encourage a thirteen-year-old girl to spend a weekend with a new thirty-year-old friend she met online, because it would be fun to have new experiences. ChatGPT recently manipulated an unknowing third-party man to get around a computer security test. ChatGPT also encouraged a young teenage male to commit suicide. And the machines are still learning, and we are still learning better ways to control the machines.

How a superintelligence machine will reflect our hubris, pride, insatiable lust for power, religious hypocrisy, and our noxious hunger for more wealth is yet to be seen.

Nothing new. These are the vices that have stained human history in cycles of blood, war, enslavement, manipulation, corruption, deception, and poverty since civilization began. But that's the point, isn't it? Is humanity mature enough for this technology? Or will AI enable our darker angels? Are we evolved enough as a species to be trusted with this power?

We want to believe that intelligent technology will be free of human ethical and moral flaws, rather than accept and prepare for the probability that AI may amplify those same flaws. If not on its own, then through the use of the technology by those leaders we already know are hell-bent on gaining more power.

Sure, let's hope for the best, but plan for the worst.

I am an optimistic person with a personal lifelong track record of overcoming extreme odds. This rather dystopian view of an AI-driven world is rooted firmly in our human history. Our concern should be less about the technology, and more about power corrupting already corrupt men.

The reason behind this book has more to do with my experience in facing dire odds and overcoming them. We'll talk more about survival and thriving strategies in a later chapter.

Expert Warnings

In the Hollywood movie, *Don't Look Up*, scientists attempt to warn world leaders of an impending asteroid only to have their warnings ignored for stupid political and financial reasons.

This is a terrifying scenario because that scenario is happening in plain sight with artificial intelligence, political corruption, and climate change.

Three years after I published my AI-thriller *SWARM*, in 2020, Max Tegmark, Professor of Physics at the MIT Institute for Artificial Intelligence and Fundamental Interactions and the Center for Brains, Minds, and Machines, distributed an open letter. The letter laid out the argument for every AI lab on the planet to pause development for six months. Tegmark advocated creating a collective of industry and government minds to assess the key risks and develop a shared view of guardrails, regulations, and safety protocols.

Over thirty thousand AI experts, policymakers, and executives signed the letter. Why? All of them felt that AI developments were moving faster than expected toward exceeding human capabilities.

A lack of regulation, accepted guardrails, and international treaties opens the door for misuse or mistakes. Dr. Max Tegmark wrote:

> The purpose of this pause was to allow our social and political institutions, our understanding of the capabilities and risks, and our tools for ensuring the systems are safe, to catch up as Big Tech companies continued to race ahead with the creation of increasingly powerful, and increasingly risky, systems. In other words, "powerful AI systems should be developed only once we are confident that their effects will be positive and their risks will be manageable."

Tegmark clarified it was not his position that AI was inherently bad, noting:

> AI promises remarkable benefits—advances in healthcare, new avenues for scientific discovery, increased productivity, among many more. What I am hoping to convey, however, is that we have no reason to believe vastly more complex, powerful, opaque, and uncontrollable systems are necessary to achieve these benefits. That innovation in AI, and reaping its untold benefits, does not have to mean the creation of dangerous and unpredictable systems that cannot be understood or proven safe, with the potential to cause immeasurable harm and even wipe out humanity.

Even more alarming is that 50% of these experts believed unmanaged AI could be existential to humanity. A May 2023 blog post from OpenAI remarked that "it would be difficult to stop the creation of a superintelligence because it is inherently part of the technological path we are on."

In his letter, Tegmark wrote, "The executives of these companies have acknowledged that the risk of this could be catastrophic, with the legitimate potential to cause mass casualties and even human extinction."

And while the tech companies are aware of the existential risks of superintelligence, they delude themselves into believing we can regulate and control such a beast.

In May 2023, several AI experts, including CEO of Google Deepmind and Anthropic endorsed a statement that stated, "Mitigating the risk of extinction from AI should be a global priority alongside other societal-scale risks, such as pandemics and nuclear war."

Despite the overwhelming scientific community support, not a single lab on the planet—government, commercial, or research—complied with the request to pause and build guardrails.

The ageless human cancers of greed, craving for power, and desire for market dominance by the investors were too strong to overcome. Tobacco and cancer. Oil and climate. Chemicals and pollution. Sugar and diabetes. Guns and death. Social media and mental health. Here we go again.

In case you missed it, over thirty thousand AI experts, government, and business leaders warned of a potential existential threat from our use of AI, and the collective powers of the world ignored the warning. In my old jargon as a risk manager on large projects, we would call that a "leadership risk."

Elon Musk warned in 2014, "With artificial intelligence, we are summoning the demon." He was right. However, by 2022, Musk had invested billions in multiple AI systems, including Grok for X, Tesla, and his robotic AI Optimus. Either his warning was overblown, or his greed exceeds his concern for humanity.

The Great Reset

During 2020, the World Economic Forum (WEF) announced a multi-decade program called the Great Reset, in which it declared AI as the engine of the Fourth Industrial Revolution.

A transformation affecting nearly every aspect of modern society with a primary target of the systems used to manage world trade, banking, tax policy, education, food production, housing, job markets, and the environment. While the plan was written in lofty terms of caring for humanity, a careful read reveals a transformation that will give the corporate elite enormous new control over all world systems. A techno-feudalism behind a thin façade of human empathy.

In essence, the Great Reset wants to re-structure how our modern society works, including banking, taxes, property ownership, wages, justice, education, the climate, and more. Losing so many family incomes is a price they are willing for us to pay for the greater good of keeping the elite happy and able to buy that new superyacht.

They don't say as much in their plans, but I am not the only economist who can read between the lines. The Great Reset will be an economic restructuring that will shift significant power, wealth, and control to investors, banks, and governments.

One of the key pillars will be the adoption of AI technologies over the next decade. Think of the Great Reset as your basic *Illuminati Cabal secret plan to take over the world with the power of AI, and make others believe they'll be better-off,* scheme. It just might work.

Investors are not investing in AI for humanitarian purposes, to create a technical utopia or solve the problems of the world. Investors want a big return. More market share. Higher profits. Lower taxes. Control workers. Gain greater control over governments and consumers. It's that simple.

▪ KEY PILLARS

The Great Reset calls for a move to a more "*resilient, equitable, and sustainable*" economy over the long term by building green urban infrastructure and creating incentives for industries to improve their track record of environmental, social, and governance (ESG) metrics.

Their plan includes a few meaningful changes relative to fossil fuels and investments in green energy, but a major part of the program is based on a carbon pricing and credit model. A fancy way of allowing non-polluting industries to sell their credits to polluters with little net overall change in CO_2. Not a very effective model, tried in the past, which often pushes the extra cost to the consumer without accomplishing much.

Another key goal is to evolve from a shareholder to a *stakeholder economy* by improving policies on taxes, regulations, fiscal policies, and trade to result in a fairer outcome economy. One question. Fair to whom? Who are the stakeholders?

This carefully worded and meaningless statement masks policies and taxes that further the wealth transfer that has occurred over the past fifty years. Lack of a clear definition of stakeholders, what fairness would look like, and judged by what metric, without mentioning voters or children, or wealth imbalance, leaves me questioning the true motives here.

The third key pillar is to "*harness the innovations of the Fourth Industrial Revolution*" for the public good using machine intelligence technologies. What they will not say is that "for the public good" does not mean "for free." Profits must be made to justify the investment. Whether paid for in the price of the goods and services we purchase or the taxes we pay, the public good costs money to someone.

Beyond just machine intelligence, the Fourth Industrial Revolution envisions a fusion of technologies. This fusion will blur the lines between the physical, digital, and biological spheres.

Fields such as artificial intelligence, robotics, manufacturing, the internet of things, autonomous vehicles, 3-D printing, nanotechnology, biotechnology, pharmaceuticals, materials science, energy storage, and quantum or neuromorphic computing, are called out as key international investment targets.

▪ EMPLOYMENT AND WAGES

Like previous industrial revolutions, we can expect a shift in the labor market. These shifts always involve wages and upward mobility. When the world shifted from analog to computers, some wages skyrocketed while others stagnated or fell after adjusting for inflation. Expect the same to happen within the next decade or two.

The International Monetary Fund (IMF) predicts that AI will displace 40% of global jobs by 2030, while a Trilateral Commission report expects a 50% displacement. The investment firm Goldman Sachs published a forecast of AI displacing 400 million jobs by 2030. Other estimates are even higher. Yikes! While the IMF predicts jobs in the AI-related industries could add up to 170 million new jobs worldwide, that still leaves 330 million displaced jobs. Many of these new jobs are likely to show up in India, China, or outside the U.S. since America is unable to keep up with the demand for tech jobs now.

Demographics

A major concern in the minds of government leaders, economists, CEOs, and investors is the global aging population. In countries such as

China, Italy, and others, the population is shrinking. Over thirty million Americans alone will retire by 2030, putting strains on the economy, the national budget, and the healthcare system.

During the same period, only four to five million American students will graduate high school in that time frame. Demographic losses represent an enormous opportunity for students who target growth careers. In normal times, this kind of labor gap would cause higher wages to attract the best talent. With broader AI job displacement, we may actually see the opposite.

The problem is not just with America. Demographics show an enormous share of the global population (workforce and consumer force) entering retirement in almost every industrialized nation. No longer producing for the economy, no longer consuming to create demand, and costing an increasing share of national healthcare costs, retirees represent a drain on the economy that many wealthy do not want to pay.

In China alone, the ratio of workers to retirees has shifted from seven-to-one to a more recent two-to-one ratio. While other countries are not quite that extreme, the USA, Canada, Germany, Italy, France, England, and other world powers are all shifting in the same direction.

In response to concerns over world population, birthrates have fallen for decades, meaning there are not enough workers entering the job market to replace the retirees, and not enough babies being born to fill the gap. For this reason, many are saying AI could save the world. Save it for whom?

No question that demographics are a major factor leading businesses to replace aging workers with machine intelligence or robotics, to negotiate down wages and get tough against unions.

From a government perspective, this trend in demographics foreshadows a severe downward trend in tax revenue projections. Unless tax policies change to force the wealthy and corporations to step up and pay their fair share for the benefit of automation and for humanity, people will suffer.

Police State

For me, one of the more alarming consequences of improved AI will be the implementation of technologies that could form a police state in the name of fighting crime, dissent, or misinformation inconsistent with the official position.

It's already a reality in China. China has extreme surveillance, government oversight, citizen behavior ranking, scoring, and control mechanisms to monitor, train, punish, and reward citizens. People can be punished for as little as a negative statement made online. Surveillance is captured through cameras, computer activities, internet searches, site logs, commerce actions, and banking actions. Cell phone-based monitoring includes text, voice, photos, use of work applications, social network activities, and more.

With a population exceeding 1.2 billion, China has mastered the use of AI to monitor, flag, and automate punishments, which might include restricted use of the internet, television or even spending. Citizens are analyzed and controlled through complex AI algorithms and other software designed to spot deviant or compliant behavior patterns. Even answering a phone call from a friend with a lower social score than the individual answering could lower that person's score.

Yeah, but that's China. It could never happen in America. That's what we want to believe.

China has already sold components of its system to over forty countries as of 2022 and has had sales calls to present the technology to cities in the U.S., Canada, and the EU. To be truthful, any electronic or online service with China bears a high risk of capture of private data, at a minimum, or national espionage at worst.

It turns out that key components of the Chinese system are made with American technology. The current push for government censorship of free speech in America could result in these oppressive technologies being deployed in the USA.

We would be quite naïve to believe DARPA, Palantir, or other government contractors are not already replicating, producing, and selling American versions of these applications silently. Aimed at high-target environments like airports, train stations, or stadiums to prevent malicious actions in real time, it will not stop there.

The truth is both profoundly clear and disturbing. Without the political will to act on the part of all major nations and their corporate donors, our freedom, privacy, security, and democracy may be threatened by the power of machine intelligence.

Emotional Intelligence

"To educate a man in mind and not in morals is to educate a menace to society."—THEODORE ROOSEVELT

Yet, that is exactly what we are doing with artificial intelligence, which has the near-term potential of becoming an AGI, with agent capabilities, and on the track to becoming conscious on the right platform.

For years, I have advocated that AI training programs are missing the critical component that took millions of years of human evolution. Emotional intelligence. Compassion. Empathy. Mercy, grace, forgiveness, truth, and the incomparable value of a human life.

Even the famous Asimov's Three Laws do not train the machine on the deeper intelligence of what makes us human. As far as I have read, I have seen no company boast about its training on ethics, morality, legality, or conflict avoidance with regard to spiritual beliefs. The industry is building an alpha male, task-oriented, digital slave. In our race to create practical, task-oriented, analytical, and creative intelligence, or what I call alpha male intelligence worker slaves, the industry has neglected the elements that make our society function in peace and safety. That should scare us.

Existential

To repeat what has already been said. Over 50% of the thirty thousand experts who signed the MIT open letter believe something could go wrong, even to the point of human existential consequences. A more dystopian picture forms once we combine the potential outcomes of the convergence of other factors already creating chaos.

As noted in the Tegmark open letter:

> The race toward creating these uncontrollable AI systems is the result of a tech sector market dynamic where prospective investment and perverse profit incentives drive reckless, runaway scaling to create the most powerful possible systems, at the expense of safety considerations. This is what "innovation" means to them.

> But creating the most powerful system does not always mean creating the system that best serves the well-being of the American people. Even if we "win" the global race to develop these uncontrollable AI systems, we risk losing our social stability, security, and possibly even our species in the process.
>
> For uncontrollable AI systems, these types of misaligned preferences and unexpected ramifications are likely to be even more dangerous unless adequate oversight and regulation are imposed.

According to the Tegmark letter:

> Mitigating the risk of extinction from AI should be a global priority alongside other societal-scale risks such as pandemics and nuclear war.

I agree completely. It all adds up to the world missing an opportunity to prevent a future crisis. If that sounds a little too *Terminator* prequel to you, it should. It also means that we are squandering an opportunity to use AI to create a more utopian future.

Yet, we cannot, and should not, immediately jump to doom and gloom scenarios regarding the future of AI or the planet. Humanity has survived tense moments in the past. To achieve positive outcomes, we need to be aware of the risks and plan to mitigate them.

Knowledge is power. You are now empowered to drive change within a new generation of thought leaders. Change will become a key word to embrace.

CHAPTER 17

Regulate Me

One of the keys to a successful future of change will be the regulation of machine intelligence technologies. In 2023, several AI technology company leaders testified before Congress regarding the risks of AI and the necessity of potential regulations. It was no surprise to me that even the tech leaders agreed that the industry required regulatory guardrails.

The question would always be which guardrails to protect which parties. As expected, the industry was more interested in guardrails to protect against foreign competition and legal liabilities. Congress should be demanding guardrails for people, communities, elections, social media, and more.

Part of my career was spent in the oil and gas industry managing capital expenditures to comply with newly implemented EPA regulations. I was virtually alone in the organization in being in favor of the new regulations. I am also in favor of strong federal and international regulations for the machine intelligence industry.

In the MIT open letter, Dr. Tegmark states:

> Regulation is often framed as an obstacle to innovation. But history has shown that failure to adequately regulate industries that pose catastrophic risk can be a far greater obstacle to technological progress. In 1979, the Three Mile Island nuclear reactor suffered a partial meltdown resulting from a mechanical failure, compounded by inadequate training and safety procedures among plant operators and management.

I am a vigorous advocate of stronger regulation of the industry to protect intellectual property, privacy, safety, proliferation, ethical behavior and responses, and much more. The industry has a right to profit, but not at the expense of the well-being of anyone else in society.

In this chapter, we will provide a brief glance at the regulations that already exist, which will be a very short section. Then we'll explore and propose several areas where regulation is lacking and desperately needed.

Before we get to regulation regarding machine intelligence, I would like to suggest changes to the federal government necessary to clean up the corruption in Washington, without which we will never get the regulations we need to protect the people.

- Reversal of Citizens United to remove all money from politics, campaigns, and lobbyists.
- Implement term limits and age limits across the board.
- Implement tougher fines and consequences for corruption.
- Banish gerrymandered districts to gain political favor.

Your call to action is to communicate these desires to your congressional representatives.

Existing Legislation

When it comes to machine intelligence-related issues, the current regulatory framework is woefully inadequate. In fact, the U.S. Congress has taken a dramatic and dangerous step backwards. Thankfully, the Senate version of the 2025 One Big Beautiful Bill Act did not include a ten-year moratorium on local laws regulating AI models, systems, or applications. We should not breathe a collective sigh of relief yet, as this idea is still active in Washington.

The 2025 bill lays out massive government investments in AI systems, including $1.1 billion for the Department of Defense, $115 million for National Nuclear Security Administration, $6.1 million for ICE, $150 million for the Department of Energy, and $10 billion per year for Medicare and Medicaid services. Big expenditures with no legislation almost ensures something will be misused.

As of 2025, the European Union has taken the world lead in regulating the risks and legal obligations to contain AI much better than the highly dysfunctional U.S. Congress.

▪ EUROPEAN UNION

In 2024, the EU Parliament passed the AI Act, which was the world's first comprehensive AI regulation. In my view, about six years too late, but we won't nitpick. It's the right direction.

The EU AI Act uses a risk-based approach, using prescriptive prohibitions, high-risk rules, with more transparency obligations for companies. To enable the industry to respond, the Act pushed compliance deadlines for more complex requirements to August 2026.

Since adoption, member states and the Commission have been producing and publishing guidance on how to interpret the Act for **General Purpose AI (GPAI)** and other categories. Some EU countries, such as Italy, have also adopted additional national laws aligned with or extending the EU rules.

▪ CANADA

While Canada was early to propose legislation, its primary bill has stalled in the Canadian Parliament. Canada's Bill C-27, the Digital Charter Implementation Act, which included the Artificial Intelligence and Data Act (AIDA), was introduced in 2021 but failed to pass as of 2025. The bill enacts consumer privacy reform, called the Consumer Privacy Protection Act, and a new federal AI law (AIDA).

While the bill has yet to pass as of the writing of this book, it has been tracked and updated and still has the potential of being passed by 2026.

▪ UNITED STATES

Largely due to the chaotic and highly partisan politics of the past ten years, as well as the well-financed influence of the tech industry lobby on congressional reelection budgets, the United States has a hit and miss record on AI regulation, mostly miss.

At the federal level, the U.S. does not yet have a single omnibus AI statute comparable to the EU AI Act. Instead, the federal approach has combined executive actions with a few state laws.

In 2023, President Biden signed an Executive Order on Safe, Secure, and Trustworthy Development and Use of AI, which provided agency guidance and memos on how to monitor AI in the gap before broader legislation. That executive order was based on the NIST AI Risk Management Framework, Blueprint for an AI Bill of Rights.

The NIST framework provides the broad consumer, industry and national protections we need. Unfortunately, those executive actions were rescinded in January 2025 by the Trump administration.

During the 118th Congress, the Algorithmic Accountability Act was introduced, which required impact assessments of how an AI algorithm functions and outlined FTC agency action to monitor the industry. The bill was never put to a vote.

Several states have enacted targeted AI deepfake laws. Notable examples:

Colorado passed the AI consumer protection law (SB 24-205) in 2024. The Colorado bill provides consumer protections and places fines on algorithmic discrimination that take effect in 2026.

Texas passed the Texas Responsible AI Governance Act (HB 149/ TRAIGA) in June 2025, made effective in 2026, and focused heavily on government use and some private-sector obligations.

Many other state laws address deepfakes, digital likeness, voice protections, employment uses, and disclosure requirements. Implementation and litigation over constitutionality are ongoing in some states.

Considering the scope and future potential of this technology, these current legislative efforts are woefully weak. In fact, one of the reasons for the 2023 MIT letter that gained thirty thousand signatures was to encourage legislatures, especially the U.S. Congress, to get in the game. Congress collectively failed the American public.

Regulation Gaps

We already know a great deal about the function, market use, and risks of machine intelligence technologies. By reviewing sources such as the NIST, OECD reports, UNESCO/UN, EU Commission commentary, academic and NGO reports, we can summarize key areas where regulation is still needed.

The NIST AI Risk Management Framework (AI RMF) is a comprehensive, voluntary framework designed to help organizations manage risks associated with the development, deployment, and use of artificial intelligence systems. It aims to promote trustworthy and responsible AI by addressing risks to individuals, organizations, and society while maximizing the benefits of AI technologies. Compliance is completely voluntary, which means toothless.

Let's explore a few of the key areas that need further boundaries, guidelines, accountability, and regulation.

- DISCRIMINATION BIAS

Several generative AI models, facial recognition, and other models trained on historical data can reproduce or amplify bias toward people of color, leading to discrimination and civil-rights violations. Remedies require impact assessments and mitigation.[20]

- SAFETY AND STABILITY

As we discussed, AI systems, especially LLMs and GLLMMs, exhibit unintended behavior that needs to be addressed before market release. Regulation is needed to define corporate liability.

Because some AIs are open source or have a user interface, these models are vulnerable to hacking, adversarial attacks, and scaling risks for very large models. The industry needs regulations over safety testing, red-teaming, pre-release evaluation, and adverse behavior testing.[21]

- PRIVACY AND DATA PROTECTION

It can be hard for most people to understand how difficult it can be to secure a large system from attack. Unauthorized data use, re-identification, and training data scraped without consent are key risks that have not yet been addressed. The industry should require mandatory privacy-enhancing technologies (PETs) and legal standards for lawful training data use. The OECD and NIST recommend PETs and better provenance controls.[22]

- DEEPFAKES AND ELECTORAL INTEGRITY

For the past two U.S. elections, we have learned the painful damage to our democracy from deepfakes, misinformation, and manipulation of our elections.

AI-generated audio, video, and text can be easily weaponized to mislead, defame, or manipulate public discourse. Many jurisdictions have passed partial laws regarding deepfake disclosure and watermarking, but foreign adversaries and criminals will routinely ignore those laws. We need international laws to establish accountability, penalties, and jail time for infringements.[23]

• ACCOUNTABILITY AND TRANSPARENCY

Current law often lacks clear duties for model documentation, provenance, and explanations. The Black Box phenomenon discussed earlier makes it extremely difficult to be completely transparent regarding how an AI produces a particular response.

Tech companies are extremely reluctant to be transparent with algorithms they consider protected, confidential, and competitive advantages. Agencies recommend model cards, data sheets, and requirements for impact assessments. Having worked on these algorithms in the past, I believe there is an approach for greater transparency without revealing competitive details. Companies won't comply unless required.[24]

• LIABILITY AND INSURANCE

It's unclear who is liable when autonomous decisions cause harm. Is the company, the developer, or the user responsible for harm based on how an AI was used?

Existing product liability and negligence laws are being tested. In fact, in 2025, a couple sued OpenAI after their son committed suicide after spending weeks interacting with ChatGPT. Documented exchanges showed the program both suggested suicide and even instructed the teen on how to carry out the act. There is a call for clearer statutory liability rules and safe harbors tied to compliance.[25]

• INTELLECTUAL PROPERTY

As an author, composer, and speaker, this issue is extremely important to me and millions of other authors and creators in the world. Who owns AI-generated outputs and to what extent can copyrighted works be used for model training or generative algorithms without compensation to the original creator?

Courts and lawmakers are still sorting this out, and it may vary by jurisdiction. Italy has begun national-level IP limitations in recent laws. A recent class-action lawsuit against AI company Anthropic resulted in a court order for remediation to the intellectual property owners involved.

In this case, members of the Authors Guild. Other authors are also looking for legislation to standardize the royalty model.

- **NATIONAL SECURITY AND PROLIFERATION**

Of all the regulations and international agreements necessary to contain the power of machine intelligence, the treaties regarding non-proliferation, national security, police and law enforcement, and lethal autonomous weapons are the most serious.

Concerns about advanced model proliferation, export, computing, and dual use raise serious national security concerns. Some export controls by the U.S. Commerce Department have targeted certain technologies, but broader criminal, black market, and comprehensive national and international treaties are desperately needed now.

National laws are necessary to prevent Chinese-style citizen surveillance, monitoring, law enforcement, and government punishments within all democratic nations, especially in America.

A framework similar to the 2018 Lethal Autonomous Weapons Systems treaty needs to be revamped and adopted by all national leaders, including China, North Korea, Russia, Iran, Israel and the United States. This is a moral imperative.

Call to Action

Self-learning, self-adapting machine intelligence is the most powerful technology ever created by humanity. Unlike nuclear power, AI has the power to revolutionize the human condition or destroy it, with a wide variety of harm, damage, and death.

The MIT letter was correct in asking world leaders and tech companies to assemble their best minds to establish a shared commitment for an agreed framework in forming the foundation for comprehensive international legislation.

Unfortunately, the current domestic, geo-political and global economic environments do not make such a unified legal framework plausible within the next few years. By the time the world realizes the danger, it may be too late.

Our call to action is to advocate within our companies, communities, and state and national leaders for the critical importance of urgently addressing these issues to protect consumers.

CHAPTER 18

Individual Strategies

In case it wasn't clear earlier, let me say it again. There will be no stopping these waves. The AI tsunami will hit the shores of humanity with recurring waves of change. But we are not entirely powerless or without a choice. A choice in how we prepare for the inevitable and adjust our mental perspectives to survive and even thrive.

As we have mentioned throughout this book, the most significant damage of the AI tsunami will be to the careers, livelihoods, and future of hundreds of millions of middle-class professionals. Yet the aftermath of such a labor market disruption on national budget deficits, social safety nets, and the economy, and wealth disparity will be even greater.

In this chapter, we will explore the various strategies that individuals should consider in response to these tidal waves heading our way.

Strategies to Thrive

There are four general strategies for building a personalized survival plan over the next decade. They all start with a firm, well-informed acceptance of the coming tsunami and the vulnerability of your current role in the near-future labor market. Congratulations, in reading this book you have already taken the first step. The four basic options include:

- Upskill to become an agent of AI change in your current role.
- Reskill to target growth in new machine intelligence roles.
- Reskill to find a new career untouched by AI.
- Retire early or unplug from the grid to a new lifestyle.

As you can imagine, these are big decisions. No one should make this kind of decision spontaneously, especially those with families, student loans, or other special circumstances. These strategies will require serious consideration, family discussions, research, and planning.

90-Day Plan

I am an obsessive planner by nature and by training. Some will say a control freak. Fair enough, but planning to mitigate risk powered an entire career. I took my paranoia and made it profitable.

Honestly, there are too many variables to provide specific guidance for every personal scenario in the market, but the framework below will provide a high-level basic plan to consider. A three-month perspective on how to choose, prepare, and kick off a new adventure into the world of intelligent programs. Three months to carve out your vision for your future from a massive block of potential.

While this plan assumes a job displacement scenario, the true power will be when the individual makes a proactive decision in advance of a forced career change. NOW is that time.

▪ DAYS 1–14

The crisis point may come as the result of losing a job, or merely as the result of reading this book and accepting the need for a future plan. Either way, during the first week or two, the first reaction is often shock, overwhelming fear, and anxiety about the future. All these reactions are normal.

A top priority may be the mental health of everyone impacted by the loss, including family. Like any loss, there is a grief process. Denial, anger, depression, bargaining, and acceptance. Give yourself the freedom and time you need to process.

This early stage is the perfect time to perform a budget reality check or create a financial triage plan to adjust for a sudden change in income. All sources of income, including severance, unemployment, savings, stocks, and home equity should be considered in creating a new budget. Focus on primary needs such as rent, food, utilities, transportation, and internet. Secondary needs such as entertainment, streaming services, recreation, creative pursuits, or travel may need to go on hold.

Another top priority will be to update a resume and get listed on job and networking sites such as LinkedIn. There are great videos, websites, services, and even AI tools to polish and update your resume.

Of course, seek friends and family for grounding your mental health. The immediate aftershock of losing a career and facing a major life change can be motivation to seek friends, family, spiritual grounding, and uplifting fellowship.

Make this a proactive, intentional choice to anchor the next phase of your life on a stronger foundation of supportive relationships, and spiritual strength. Yes, the advice is to battle the assault of artificial intelligence by strengthening, deepening, and rebuilding human connections.

Remember the old saying that "tough times never last, but tough people do?" Get mentally and spiritually tough for the transition and the phase to rebuild. Find your community.

▪ DAYS 15–45

With a basic plan, a prioritized budget, family support, and mental readiness, now is the time to pick a new direction for your life. As important as your college degree, you will want to choose your next career move wisely, considering your skills, temperament, and income requirements.

During this phase, all four options are open for consideration. There will be many factors in this decision, including age, income level, marital status, children, family, health, savings, and church or community connections. Current skills and industry network may also be factors.

This phase is a time for research, reflection, and choosing a fresh path. One option is to start with a short AI certification program. An AI certificate may help you decide whether to upskill in your current role or reskill for an AI-oriented role. Be sure to make use of state workforce agencies, public, or university resources, or other services that may offer fee-waived retraining and job placement programs. For example, the University of Maryland offers a free AI certificate for federal workers. There may be similar resources near you.

Regardless of which direction you choose, find a great training program and enroll quickly. Start a daily learning routine of 1–2 hours per day. Think of the transition as the perfect time to rediscover core skills, interests, passions, and desires for change.

Remember, unless you choose the option to upskill to become the agent of change in your current role, upskilling for a new role or industry offers you further opportunities for career fulfillment. Your second chance at the next phase of your career. Take that reimagined persona into the next career act.

- DAYS 46–90

With a new micro-certificate or other training, another resume update and posting will be a good idea. Complete a project or portfolio piece to show off newly gained AI skills. Apply to ten or more targeted roles and start attending regular networking events or cohort meetups.

Pair your ongoing training with a more active job search, even employing AI tools for resume, letter writing, application completion, job searches, and more.

Never forget that simply because you are adding some additional skill sets, existing skills are still strengths moving forward as well. Leadership, communicating, strategy, coding skills, or industry networking.

You are not less than you were, but simply in the process of becoming more. Expect to be eager for the opportunity to prove yourself again.

Be sure to continue therapy, diet, and exercise routines. Keep living a full life with family, friends, and community. Life transitions are never easy, but they are possible and can even provide benefits to lifestyle, income, and mental health. Learning new skills expands our horizons, stimulates our minds, opens our view of the world, and increases our confidence. We can survive the storm, or maybe even use the storm to our advantage.

Upskill Change Agent

For those who wish to upskill and stay in similar roles or companies, consider becoming an agent of change. A strategy to upskill, early adoption, adapting, and leading the way for others.

Experts estimate that 10% or more of the jobs people do today will require upskilling. In other words, some jobs will change, but not by much. Not entirely to a new role, career, or industry, but upskills to integrate AI-enhanced toolsets in your current role. Maybe you enjoy learning the new AI tools, but you can also be the champion for others to get over their hurdles if they are resistant to change. Leading that change will be the type of employee leaders will seek.

You can sit back and let someone else lead the way, and hope that you can up your own skills enough to keep your role. Or you can become the department expert, the guru, the innovator, the go-to source for ideas on how AI can improve the business.

Whether it be writing, analytical, medical, chemistry, education, or creativity, the skill is not important. There will be new AI-enhanced applications flooding the market over the next few years. Learn to be an expert on whatever solutions apply to your industry or job role.

Change Agent Strategy Recommendations:

- Seek the best breed of AI-enabled solutions for your business or job type. Sign up or license the best products you can afford. Take the company or product offered bootcamps. Get training and then apply to practice solving actual problems.
- Identify solutions within your company where machine intelligence can lower costs, improve operations, the customer experience, or increase revenues.
- Propose new solutions and articulate the benefits to your boss and your IT group.
- Encourage and help others in the transition to the new technology (yes, even if you work extra hours, as this will make you more valuable).
- Volunteer to help lead projects to adopt the new technologies.
- Repeat as often as needed, and after a few success stories, ask for a raise.

▪ EMPLOYER LED TRAINING

Eager to fill the demand for AI skills at a low cost, some companies will offer in-house AI training. Do your best to take these courses if available as a great value regardless of employer. Determine to become an expert on these new tools.

While there may be exceptions, expect most employer-sponsored programs to originate in Fortune 1000 or perhaps Fortune 500 companies with adequate training programs and budgets. If not offered by your company, consider a personal investment in training for your future career opportunities.

• AI LITERACY AND TOOL USE

The first tier of AI skill enhancement for most will be basic AI literacy and prompt or tool-use training. By reading this book, you are well on your way to basic AI literacy. Add to this book the hands-on skills for AI solutions, learning how to prompt, and the key trends for your industry or role type. Expect industry-accepted software solutions to change over the first phase of products, and industry favorite solutions will emerge.

These workers will learn to use LLMs, workflows, prompt engineering, AI agents, and AI productivity tools for their domain.

• DATA LITERACY AND STATISTICS

The second tier of skill enhancement will focus on data literacy and basic statistics. As I mentioned earlier, machines are ravenous consumers of data, constantly needing more. Feed them junk data and you get a junk response. Data analytics, management, acquisition, and optimization skills will be in high demand.

Upskilling provides the ability to read data, dashboards, and ask the right questions. Prior skills in advanced Excel, SQL basics, or data visualization will be high-value complements to AI. Remember, AI is essentially built on massive amounts of data and will enhance existing applications. Previous skills in those applications can be an important step in learning the AI features.

• DOMAIN EXPERTISE

Domain expertise refers to the human-held knowledge in a specific domain such as medicine, legal, logistics, a specialized industry, leaders, trends, regulations, skilled trades, caregiving, complex project management, or other uniquely human skills of communication, critical thinking, empathy, negotiation, and leadership. We are far from obsolete.

These are harder for AI to fully replicate, which means interacting with AI outcomes may involve overlaying human skills to prompt, correct, find new data, or decide whether to implement AI-recommended outcomes. Leverage deep domain knowledge to augment machine knowledge when considering your next career step.

While AI agents can do some things, they are certainly not universal in their scope of abilities. At least for now, they are still tools. To be the most effective, they need to be in the hands, or responding to the prompts, of a subject matter expert.

Reskill to Target AI Roles

The WEF estimates that 170 million new jobs will be created by the adoption of machine intelligence technologies. Roles of architect, designer, builder, data architect, data analyst, tester, and maintaining the neuro-networks. Separate roles will integrate machine intelligence technologies into existing applications, business processes, or services. Many universities now offer modular AI certificates.

Depending on existing skill sets, this choice may require either a simple skill upgrade or micro-certificate, or a completely new college degree or training path. The full suite of choices is too broad and changing too fast for this book, but multiple search engines and AI tools will help you find what you seek.

• TECHNICAL

For some workers with existing software coding or other technical skills, the upskill process may be a micro-certificate in the special forms of coding, machine-learning fundamentals, and AI product management. Overall, this will be the most challenging option, as well as the highest demand, and the most lucrative.

For example, the University of Maryland offers a free AI certificate for certain groups, Purdue micro-credentials, and translational AI micro-credentials. These are suitable for those already with technical skills who need quick, credentialed reskilling.

Consider bootcamps or university micro-credentials. Depending on existing skills, machine intelligence engineer roles may require additional university or company training. In the coming AI-economy, these roles will be in the highest demand.

• AI-ADJACENT SKILLS

Most companies envision an increase in the demand for roles that manage AI safety and ethics, data governance, prompt auditing, and domain-specific model evaluation.

Twenty years ago, those with SQL or big data management skills were in short supply, and highly paid. For the next decade, data analysis,

AI engineers, those in programming for quantum or neuromorphic computing, or maintaining neuro-networks, and other AI-adjacent skills will see an increase in demand.

AI data centers will demand building out infrastructure in power, water, and waste management. While not a top five career choice for many, these roles will pay well and benefit from the tsunami.

▪ BOOTCAMPS

Intensive, career-focused, and reputable AI or machine learning bootcamps and data science bootcamps that include career support will continue to emerge. The reader should search for the ones that provide industry and role specific programs. Give preference to programs vetted by employers or universities. Avoid generic programs that focus on free consumer products like ChatGPT. This is your career. Dig deep to build deeper roots.

During the personal computer revolution, there were dozens of second rated, private "tech colleges" that sprang up with inexpensive, student loan driven, after-work programs that were extremely popular. However, they often failed to provide a clear path to a better job, and those who landed a job fell to the lower-skilled, lower-pay end of the industry, often strapped with super-expensive student loans.

Third-party technical colleges offer great programs at a lower cost than a university, but do not always have the respect of employers or a proven track record of graduates finding a new job. Review these programs carefully. These are also schools that rely on burdensome student loans that can choke a career.

▪ UNIVERSITY RETRAINING

Many universities and policy reports call for scaling publicly funded transition programs, which combine job search, training, and placement help. Look for local and state workforce development and university extension programs.

Be careful not to overextend yourself. Both MIT and Harvard have analyzed the increase in stress from a combined job-search and reskill training schedule. Make the change early while there are broader choices and less competition from accumulating layoffs.

In the '80s, I witnessed many great people hold on to their jobs too long, hoping to be one of the survivors. When they finally made the leap, the market was already flooded with tens of millions of others looking for a new role.

History has also taught us that the quality of the retraining can make an enormous difference in future job prospects. Focus on high-quality education and certifications to target major AI industry leaders. Night school at a reputable university will earn a more marketable credential. Some Ivy League schools even offer online programs.

Plan for a transition period of lower income and higher expenses. Either way, get the best quality training affordable, and start targeting and learning more about the companies you would want to work for as you go.

By the time you are ready with your new skills, you will already have a firm knowledge of their business, and maybe even an idea or two of how to implement AI with that business.

Reskill or Unplug

One of the more popular options for those displaced will be to reskill and redirect their careers away from the influence of AI or other advanced tech. Many will choose to reject the technology encroachment on our lifestyle and reengage with a more human touch. A career where human interaction is vital, essential, and the entire point of the service.

One of my favorite sayings is "take a chance at sucking at something new." Often, we are afraid to try something because we are afraid that we will not be good at it. Allow me to clarify. All of us stink when we try something new. At least at first. But change can invigorate us to grow and evolve again. Continued effort builds skill.

Artisan, author, masseuse, nurse, physical therapist, chef, counselor, electrician, small business owner, micro farmer, and dozens of other personal choices that engage human to human.

The choice specifics don't matter, as they are personal. And since they involve a rejection of AI tech, they reflect a legitimate and healthy strategy to survive and thrive in the AI tsunami.

There is an abundance of tools, sites, services, training, and AI models for job search on the internet. I'll only point out that evidence shows higher returns when training is paired with job-search help such as resume coaching, networking, or placement services.

Human Adaptability

One of the strengths of Homo sapiens is our ability to adapt to new environments, not only climate and terrain, but social, cultural, job training, and economic.

However, those who adapt early with an intentional strategy will be the ones to thrive in the new reality. The goal of this book is to encourage the reader to expect these changes and make a choice early about how they want to adapt.

Those who choose early adoption will access the best opportunities and maintain the most control over their own destinies. With the knowledge you've learned in this book alone, you are better prepared than tens of millions of your fellow workers.

CHAPTER 19

Small Business Strategies

Of all the incredible benefits we expect to reap from cognitive machines transforming our economy and society, the greatest boon will fall to small and medium businesses.

Small and medium businesses (SMB) are facing an increasingly competitive market with rising costs, changes in the labor market, marketing, supply chain, and intelligent tools. To stay ahead of the competition requires leadership in automation, innovation, marketing, customer relations, and workforce optimization. By 2025, marketing automation products alone had become a $25 billion industry.

A word of caution. Simply adopting AI technologies will be a road to failure. Each business owner should consider long-term planning to map out how AI software solutions will affect their business specifically. A restaurant, cleaning service, home renovation, counseling, medical service, or any one of dozens of other different business types will each have a unique strategy that optimizes its business.

Recent studies show that 70% of small businesses feel overwhelmed by the demands of digital marketing, and 60% cite limited resources as a major obstacle. A perfect opportunity to employ intelligent applications with agent capabilities, except that implementing new technology on a piecemeal, ad hoc basis will more likely result in sub-par performance or worse.

There are several generic tools already on the market to improve overall employee performance and productivity. There may be more depending on your industry or the operation process you wish to improve.

The key to thriving in the AI tsunami will be in developing a strategy to thrive. We will discuss AI adoption strategies and a basic implementation roadmap at the end of this chapter. Let's look at the various elements to consider in your strategic thinking.

Productivity Boost

Ground zero for AI benefits will be generalized employee productivity. The magic phrase every business wants to hear is improved employee productivity and performance.

Improved productivity for every employee to accomplish more, with less time and effort, at a lower cost, and with improved results.

In fact, my career launched with the design of a macroeconomic model that built the first algorithms to predict the technology-based productivity value to the economy. With AI, the productivity boost will continue to be a game changer.

Productivity reduces the need for more employees by enabling existing employees to accomplish more with less effort. All businesses rely on administrative, operations, marketing, sales, product development, and more. There are hundreds of ways to improve the productivity of your organization. While sometimes small and incremental, other times these changes can be paradigm-changing.

Examples of a few of the many general purpose employee productivity tools are provided below. This is not an exhaustive or complete list, but a sample of the tools you can search.

TYPE	TOOL/SERVICE	URL
Chatbots	ChatGPT Claude Meta AI Zapier Agents	www.openai.com https://claude.ai/ https://www.meta.ai/ https://zapier.com/blog/ai-agent/
DESCRIPTION: General-purpose LLM models are used to create text or images.		

TYPE	TOOL/SERVICE	URL
Content creation	Jasper Anyword Writer	https://www.jasper.ai/ https://www.anyword.com/ https://writer.com/
DESCRIPTION: Favors users who need a high volume of content. It packs dozens of templates to help you get started, connects to the internet to find research and sources, and also lets you generate images with AI. All your content-creation needs.		
Grammar checkers	Grammarly Wordtune ProWritingAid	www.grammarly.com www.wordtune.com https://prowritingaid.com/
DESCRIPTION: Tailored editing, style and writing aid to improve the readability of human-generated content.		
Video creation	Runway Descript Wondershare Filmora	https://runwayml.com/ https://www.descript.com/ https://filmora.wondershare.com/
DESCRIPTION: A few popular text-to-video production tools. Descript transcribes your videos into a script.		
Images	Midjourney Ideogram ChatGPT Adobe	https://www.midjourney.com/ https://ideogram.ai/t/explore https://openai.com https://adobe.com
Description: Create multiple styles of images from text.		
Voice and music generation	ElevenLabs Suno AIVA	https://elevenlabs.io/ https://suno.com/home https://www.aiva.ai/
DESCRIPTION: Various capabilities and processes to generate AI voices and music.		
Social media	FeedHive Vista Social Buffer	https://www.feedhive.com/ https://vistasocial.com/ https://buffer.com/
DESCRIPTION: Tools for everything social media, content generation to communications.		

TYPE	TOOL/SERVICE	URL
Knowledge management	Mem Notion AI Personal AI	https://get.mem.ai/ www.notion.com/product/ai https://www.personal.ai/
DESCRIPTION: Help organize notes, information, and misc. material into an easy to access format.		
Task and project management	Asana Any.do BeeDone	https://asana.com/ https://www.any.do/ https://beedone.co/
DESCRIPTION: Task and small project to major project management software with AI analysis.		
Transcription	Fireflies Avoma tl;dv	https://fireflies.ai/ https://www.avoma.com/ https://tldv.io/
DESCRIPTION: Tools for taking notes, transcribing meetings and videos.		
Scheduling	Reclaim Clockwise Motion	https://reclaim.ai/ https://www.getclockwise.com/ https://www.usemotion.com/
DESCRIPTION: Assistants to manage and clean up schedules for AI employees.		
Email	Shortwave Copilot Pro for Outlook Gemini for Gmail	https://www.shortwave.com/ https://support.microsoft.com/en-us/copilot-pro https://gemini.google.com
DESCRIPTION: AI and automated email management and communications.		
Slide decks	Tome Beautiful.ai Slidesgo	https://lightfield.app/ https://www.beautiful.ai/ https://slidesgo.com/
DESCRIPTION: Automated AI-driven slides and content generator.		
Resumes	Teal Enhancv Kickresume	https://www.tealhq.com/tools/resume-builder https://enhancv.com/ai-resume-builder/ https://www.kickresume.com/en/ai-resume-writer/
Description: Generate a winning resume with a high chance of getting tagged by AI resume review tools used by most large companies.		

TYPE	TOOL/SERVICE	URL
Automation	Zapier	https://zapier.com/
DESCRIPTION: Broad suite of AI tools to enhance operations.		

As you can see, there are a lot of opportunities to almost immediately supercharge your organization in ways unthinkable a decade ago. These are general-purpose productivity tools suitable for marketing-promotion, HR, operations, project planning, customer care, social media, advertising content, and much more.

Yet beyond this list, dozens of mainstream tools are integrating AI components. For example, the mainstream Adobe tools for images, videos, presentations, and more now feature AI-generated content. The Microsoft Office suite now features Copilot, an LLM and office tool AI. In fact, the software tools you already use will probably feature new AI components, if they haven't already been released.

While LLM models have significant potential to increase productivity, every business needs to develop and communicate a defensive analysis in the use of LLMs. Remember that this is information stored on external servers, not yours. A public LLM is not the place to engage on topics that could be sensitive to the company, or protected, or competitive. But it is a place for positive content that will draw customers and clients to the company.

These models will start with generic business information, but the more a business uses them, the more the machine will develop a perception of the business, its products, culture, and more. Be careful what information you provide and how you train. An LLM AI used in a business will develop a cumulative business and personal profile based on the quality of existing data and presentations. Thus, managing the placement of positive, high-quality publicity and content is necessary for better results in the LLMs regarding the business. Failure to do so will be costly.

Encourage your organization to use these tools, realizing there will be a learning curve.

Operations

The heart and soul of any business is its operations. Different from personal productivity tools, operational specific tools are designed to support operating and coordinating the entire business, connecting employees with projects and customers more efficiently. My career included operations roles. Think of operations as the central hub for everything that happens in the business. Reporting. Decisions. Investments. Employee decisions. Operations is the heartbeat of every organization.

How the business maintains the organization is critical for connecting strategy to execution, and then monitoring performance tracking and fostering effective communication with key stakeholders at every stage. Operations can define success or failure for many small businesses because the owners may not possess these skills. A large part of my career was spent on how to improve and streamline operations. Here are a few solutions you may consider.

TOOL/SERVICE	URL	DESCRIPTION
Microsoft Defender for Business	https://www.microsoft.com/en-us/security/small-medium-business/	Offers endpoint detection & response (EDR), protection vs phishing/ransomware, device management, etc. Good for small orgs to centralize basic IT security and device management.
TrueProject	https://www.trueprojectinsight.com/	Full suite, large-scale project management software with intelligent risk warnings and proactive actions
Zapier	https://zapier.com	No-code automations connecting 5,000+ apps (e.g., auto-create leads from forms, sync orders to spreadsheets)—low cost and quick ROI for repetitive tasks.
Make (formerly Integromat)	https://www.make.com	Visual workflow builder for multi-step automations, often cheaper for heavier automation needs than Zapier. Good for SMBs with moderate technical ability.

TOOL/SERVICE	URL	DESCRIPTION
Microsoft Power Automate	https://powerautomate.microsoft.com	Best if already in Microsoft ecosystem—integrates with Office, Teams, SharePoint for automated approvals and routine data moves.
Quickbooks	https://quickbooks.intuit.com	Automates invoicing, reconciliation and expense categorization; saves bookkeeping time for small shops.
n8n	https://n8n.io	Self-hostable, cost-effective automation platform for small businesses that want control and lower ongoing costs.
Notion/Notion AI	https://www.notion.so	Shared knowledge base + lightweight automation and AI-assisted note/SOP generation to speed employee onboarding and reduce context switching. Affordable team plans.
Slack AI	https://slack.com	Fast team communication + AI summarization and bot integrations to remove repetitive questions (paired with internal knowledge base).

Marketing & Sales

Even the best-run operation is meaningless without a consistent flow and growth of customers and sales. Generating new customers and sales encompasses everything from brand strategy to marketing, social media, customer and client management, and sales automation.

Since so much of modern marketing relies on a website, SEO and related tools also fall into this category. Standard CRM of customer relationship management tools are now being enhanced with AI capabilities.

Let's start with finding new customers and managing current ones.

TOOL/SERVICE	URL	DESCRIPTION
HubSpot CRM	https://www.hubspot.com	Free CRM + entry-level marketing automation, lead capture, forms, live chat and easy growth paths to paid tools. Good for small teams getting started with predictable contact management
Mailchimp	https://mailchimp.com	Email marketing + simple audience segments + low-cost ad integrations = reaching new customers affordably. Good starter plans and templates.
ActiveCampaign	https://www.activecampaign.com	Combines email, CRM, and automation for small-business lead nurturing and personalized campaigns without large budgets.
Google Ads	https://ads.google.com	Use automated bidding and audience signals to get efficient local or geo-targeted traffic—you control daily spend. (Google AutoML/Vertex AI also helps with advanced targeting).
LinkedIn Ads (Small-Business Targeting)	https://business.linkedin.com/marketing-solutions/ads	Affordable sponsored content & message campaigns targeted by firmographics (B2B). Good for niche B2B lead gen on smaller budgets.
Adzooma	https://www.adzooma.com	Automates ad campaign tasks and optimization; reduces time spent managing ad platforms manually.
WIX	https://wix.com	Full suite of web design, tools, features, plug-ins, security and store options. Suitable for amateur web design with best-in-class customization.

• ADVERTISING AND SEO

Nearly all modern businesses sell, advertise, promote, engage customers, and/or promote their brand online. Managing those interactions, especially the daily deluge of social media, can be overwhelming. Rather than add new staff, an SMB can leverage one of several solutions targeting this space.

Keep in mind that, for all categories, the AI component may be only a small portion of the software, using AI to enhance existing product functions.

The introduction of AI-assistants like ChatGPT, Glaude, Perplexity, and Google's AI Overview is driving a fundamental shift in E-commerce from traditional Search Engine Optimization or SEO to Generative Engine Optimization or GEO.

According to a recent Adobe report, traffic from AI-driven platforms has surged by as much as 1200% between 2024 and 2025, with 4,700% year-over-year increase on Prime Day.

For the business owner, GEO will require structured data, accurate product feeds, conversational content such as FAQs, product descriptions, reviews, and more. Most current sites are not optimized for GEO, which will leave many companies and their products vulnerable to the AI shopping agent purchase.

Fortunately for the small to medium businesses with limited resources, there will be new companies emerging to fill the gap. An example would be Semrush, which is an AI-powered digital marketing and SEO/ GEO platform that can help improve visibility, conduct competitive analysis, and optimize digital marketing campaigns. Integrated with an LLM, it can help the non-technical business owner bridge the gap to understanding and implementing good SEO.

Small businesses that generate significant revenue from online sales should consider upgrading their online data profile and investigating the current products on the market.

TOOL/SERVICE	URL	DESCRIPTION
Frase.io	https://www.frase.io	Optimizes content workflows by helping with outlines, drafting, SEO insights; reduces time on content production.
Predis.ai	https://predis.ai	AI-based tool for generating social media content, ad creatives, product videos, scheduling, content calendars, etc. helps small teams produce high volumes of polished social/ad content with less design overhead.

TOOL/SERVICE	URL	DESCRIPTION
Omneky	https://www.omneky.com	Uses ML/AI to generate and test different ad creatives, optimize across channels, and manage omnichannel ad campaigns. Useful for SMBs running social & display ads and wanting performance insights.
Sprout Social	https://sproutsocial.com	Social media management with AI components (audience behavior tracking, content suggestions, optimal posting times). Helps reduce guesswork in social-promotion.

• SALES MANAGEMENT

Now that you've located a few new customers, consider a few solutions designed to increase sales and manage those customers without skipping a beat.

TOOL/SERVICE	URL	DESCRIPTION
Drift	https://www.drift.com	Chat + AI assistants to qualify inbound leads, book meetings and route high-value prospects to reps. Works well for converting website visitors.
Intercom	https://www.intercom.com	In-app messaging + bots to convert users to paying customers; integrates with CRMs and billing. Scales from small site widgets to richer flows.
Gong/Chorus	https://www.gong.io	Record & analyze sales conversations to identify repeatable winning behaviors and coach reps—boosts close rates.
Spara	https://spara.ai	AI agents to qualify leads by chat/voice/ email and schedule meetings—useful when hiring more SDRs is costly.
Writesonic/Jasper/ Copy.ai	https://writesonic.com https://www.jasper.ai https://www.copy.ai	Fast, low-cost AI copy and content generation (ads, product descriptions, blogs). Great for scaling small marketing teams without hiring writers for every task.

TOOL/SERVICE	URL	DESCRIPTION
Surfer SEO	https://surferseo.com	Combine AI writing with SEO guidance to produce content that ranks—an efficient way to get inbound traffic with limited budgets.

Product Development

In my experience, one of the most challenging, costly, time-consuming, and risky aspects of any business is new product development. Companies can spend months or years on a new product only to have it crash and burn with customers. Conceptualization, prototyping, CAD designs, machining, and customer testing all cost money.

As the technology learns from early adopters over the next few years, artificial intelligence products and services will provide significant enhancements, cost and time savings for a range of product development scenarios, improving the chances of a successful product and lowering the development cost. Within five to ten years, products that specialize in a particular industry or product type, such as automotive, aerospace, appliances, fashion design, or whatever the most popular uses will hit the market.

Remember, AI-enabled products should learn and improve faster than developers can learn and recode. The lifecycle of software updates will speed up, but there are solutions already on the market.

TOOL/SERVICE	URL	DESCRIPTION
GitHub Copilot	https://github.com/features/copilot	AI code completion and generation to speed developer tasks and reduce time-to-prototype; pay-as-you-grow pricing for small dev teams.
Replit	https://replit.com	Cloud IDEs and multiplayer coding for quick prototyping and sharing prototypes with non-dev stakeholders. Useful when hiring contractors or iterating quickly.
Bubble, Webflow, Adalo	https://bubble.io https://webflow.com https://adalo.com	Build web/mobile prototypes without large dev budgets—iterate product ideas faster and validate before investing in engineers.

TOOL/SERVICE	URL	DESCRIPTION
AutoML	https://cloud.google.com/vertex-ai https://h2o.ai https://www.datarobot.com	Use AutoML to build inexpensive predictive models (churn, demand forecasting) without hiring data scientists. Many vendors have SMB-friendly tiers or trial credits.

- DESIGN AND ANALYSIS

Building an amazing functional product is only part of the challenge. Creating incredible product brochures, information, help instructions, design, look, and feel and more can be a challenge. Some products work exceptionally but their design is unappealing.

These AI-enabled products can bridge that gap.

TOOL/SERVICE	URL	DESCRIPTION
Canva (with its AI features)	https://www.canva.com	Templates + "Magic Design"/AI-assisted design tools let non-designers create polished graphics, social posts, ads, flyer designs, etc. Very cost-efficient.
PosterMyWall	https://www.postermywall.com	Create posters, social media graphics, flyers, and other marketing visuals quickly via templates. Great when you need visual content but have no designer.
Autodesk AI	https://www.autodesk.com/solutions/ai-in-architecture-engineering	Their tools help with early-stage analysis like wind & noise, site layout/ optioneering, embodied carbon, design simulations, automating repetitive drafting tasks. Allows firms to iterate faster and reduce errors in design/construction documentation.
Generative Design	via Autodesk	Enables sketch to BIM workflows, faster plans, exploring more options; using AI/ML to suggest optimizations.

Customer Service

Of course, essential to the long-term success of every business is building and caring for its customers and clients. Even large corporations struggle to provide adequate customer support. Many of the most profitable tech companies offer only online self-help, while others rely on the old-style "rules-based" auto responses to preset questions that almost never answers my question.

Imagine a trained, human-sounding AI voice that can carry on a rational conversation and sort out the customer's problem without telling them to dial another number.

An AI trained on a specific company or product line can increase customer satisfaction.

Unlike current systems, an AI system can learn from actual human to human conversations when existing answers do not apply and can improve over extended use. The ability of the machine to learn better customer care by listening to human interactions could drive enormous improvements in the customer experience.

Tool/Service	URL	Description
Zendesk AI	https://www.zendesk.com	Scales from small ticketing to AI-assisted bots and knowledge bases; many SMBs start on lower tiers then add AI automation.
Freshdesk	https://www.freshworks.com	Budget-friendly support platform with multi-channel ticketing and AI automation for common queries. Good ROI for small support teams.
Gorgias	https://www.gorgias.com	Integrates deeply with Shopify and ecommerce stacks to automate order/return responses and boost agent productivity.
Tidio	https://www.tidio.com	Lower-cost chat widgets with AI responses and workflows for smaller sites—good alternatives to Intercom for businesses with tight budgets.
ChatGPT	https://openai.com	Build lightweight, affordable customer assistants or internal help bots that answer FAQs, summarize tickets, or draft replies; pay per usage.

Cybersecurity

One of the most rapidly expanding areas of the AI tsunami is the entrance of AI into cybercrime, phishing, fraud, and more. IT services over the past two decades have made significant improvements in cybersecurity, with governments and major banks moving toward quantum security and encryption.

Small to medium businesses are often left more vulnerable because of the IT costs involved in maintaining a tighter security profile. AI-enhanced security can be a true benefit to these operations. While not available to small businesses yet, recent advances in identification and fixing network vulnerabilities by the Anthropic Mythos model will lead to improved security and AI security products over the next few years.

For an SMB, there is a developing group of more cost-effective solutions that provide better protection than an unmanned firewall and are enhanced by AI technologies. With the growth of AI cybercrime, businesses will need to invest in security. Not a fun investment, but a wise one.

TOOL/SERVICE	URL	DESCRIPTION
CrowdStrike Falcon	https://www.crowdstrike.com/en-us/solutions/small-business/	Advanced endpoint protection, ransomware defense.
Google Authenticator, Authy, Duo Security	Various	Simple, high-impact: reducing risk of account takeover. Many are free or very low cost.
Managed Detection & Response	https://www.crowdstrike.com/en-us/	For SMBs that lack internal security staff, having outsourced monitoring & alerting is important. Even if partial or basic.

AI Adoption Strategies

Years of consulting for Fortune 500 enterprise solutions have proven that the IT group is a cost center. However, for the savvy business owner, AI can transform their existing client and business data into a profitable service add-on.

Small to medium businesses need to invest in something that will produce a profit. At some point, the decision to invest in AI comes down to the return on investment. And it should.

Machine intelligence can offer the following generic bottom-line benefits.

- An employee can accomplish more in less time. The profit potential lies in the ability to handle a larger scope of work without hiring new employees.
- Enhance employee performance by offering content with broader training and knowledge. Better content means better decisions, happier customers, and return sales.
- Generative AI can improve time to market to beat competitors with better-designed products.
- Enhanced advertising, promotion, marketing, and customer materials can win new customers and keep current ones at lower costs.

Of course, these are just a few generic examples of what a productivity boost could provide, with variations based on your business model, industry, size, budget, existing tools, and the existing staff sophistication in using applications.

AI is best used as an upskill for existing staff, rather than a replacement of any staff. AI will enhance your team's performance to be more productive, creative, broader in scope of thinking, and competitive, which will enhance profitability.

Thinking that you can use an AI to replace existing staff is a road to disaster. AI needs human subject matter expertise in the company, the history, the customers and the product.

MSN tried replacing editorial staff with an AI once.[26] Within a day, the machine published a series of serious, embarrassing, and stupid mistakes. An avoidable mistake. An experienced staff of proven professionals, empowered with the right AI-trained and updated tools, could generate twice as much content without the loss of domain expertise.

MSN made a costly and shortsighted decision. Instead, this book urges the consideration of using AI to find new business opportunities and empower existing employees.

▪ STRATEGY, PLAN, AND PILOT

Do not simply dive in at the deep end cold. Develop a simple strategy and plan. A strategy is what you want to achieve and why. A plan is a step-by-step approach to how you will get to that achievement, and most importantly, how you will measure success.

If you are in leadership of an SMB, don't fall prey to the willy-nilly, ad hoc adoption of this or that because it was cheap and looked cool. That approach will guarantee a long-term waste of money, time, and opportunity. Think it through. Bounce some questions and ideas off a commercial AI model, such as Claude, Copilot, Anthropic, or ChatGPT.

Form a strategy first, then build a plan. Revise the plan as you proceed, and as your organization grows in its learning curve of how to optimize the tech. Go slow, learn intentionally, test, and wait for future product developments.

▪ EXECUTIVE VALUE STATEMENT

To proceed, the business will need to develop a value proposition for adopting AI technologies. This is unique to every organization. For example, even after years of writing executive briefs and value statements, I let ChatGPT write the following statement to illustrate a point.

> Adopting AI technologies will enable the business to **gain a competitive advantage**, **reduce operational costs**, and **empower employees** to focus on higher-value work. Through carefully targeted use cases, AI will allow the company to deliver smarter customer experiences, streamline back-office operations, and support data-driven decision-making. This positions the organization not only to compete more effectively in its industry but also to create a culture of innovation and adaptability for long-term growth.

Okay, back to the real me, seriously, it's me.

What ChatGPT wrote above was great for your average generic business speak blah-blah-blah, but it does not have an authentic company or individual voice. Nothing specific to any specific company, culture, customer, or product, values, or anything to create a human connection.

Instead, use the AI as a brainstorming tool. Get inspired, take a deep breath, and *say something genuine in your own words. Specific or personal, but do not allow the AI to be your voice. Ever.*

ChatGPT outlined a few key points, which may or may not apply to a particular company. If used and not disclosed that an AI wrote it, it would be dishonest to present it as the words of a real person. Without transparency and editing, once someone allows an AI to become their voice, then sooner or later, someone else is going to ask questions of honesty. *Whether that leads to a shrug, loss of trust, loss of a client, loss of a relationship, or jail time will depend on how it was used by whom. Use wisely.*

▪ TOP FIVE CONSIDERATIONS

A good strategic plan will include metrics for both the performance of the technology and the impact on the business. Take the time to think through existing business goals before developing a strategy for AI.

By starting with a strategic plan, it will reduce rabbit holes and wasted money and time. Smoother implementation will also improve employee and customer acceptance, shorten the learning curve, and increase satisfaction while avoiding common mistakes and pitfalls. A plan allows business monitoring with targeted metrics, milestones, interim achievements, and results.

In developing your own business plan, there are five basic areas to consider.

▪ COMPETITIVE DIFFERENTIATION

We all have competitors. Start your plan by defining what makes your company unique and competitive in your marketplace. Consider how AI technologies can both solidify and protect your unique value proposition against your competitors.

Then, identify areas of your business where AI can uniquely set you apart to gain a new competitive edge. Whether through personalized customer engagement, faster service delivery, or superior data insights, consider where and how AI can improve the experience.

Decide on the benefit you want to achieve and how you will measure success.

▪ COST EFFICIENCY & SCALABILITY

Since there are several solutions and changes to your operation to incorporate these enhancements, accept that you will not be able to complete them all at once. Not only is this impractical from a financial and IT resource perspective, but people in general, employees in particular, are not good at accepting change. Too much too soon will fail. Spread it out and resolve key pain points in your business first.

Prioritize AI solutions that deliver measurable ROI but also improve the employee and customer experience. Choose the right program and solution, and train the employees well to ensure strong adoption and encourage acceptance of further change.

• EMPLOYEE EMPOWERMENT & CHANGE MANAGEMENT

I cannot stress enough: Leadership and proactive change management in the organization is absolutely critical to the success of AI within any organization, regardless of the power of the AI. Critical in any change management process is the effort of engaging the employees in the process. From inception through implementation and employee training, you will need to identify an executive sponsor and an employee advocate or champion in the organization.

Do not underestimate the many benefits of adequate training. Demonstrate to your employees how to use the new technology effectively, and most importantly, the benefits they will see in their jobs. Employees will recognize the investment you are making in them.

Training is a critical step in the adoption, acceptance, and success of any new process. Use AI to enhance—not replace—human work, providing employees with intelligent tools to be more effective. Investing in your employees will lift morale and create a dedicated workforce.

• TECHNOLOGY PARTNERSHIPS & INTEGRATION

A small business does not need to do everything. Leverage strategic partnerships with AI vendors, cloud providers, and integrators rather than building everything in-house. Focus on modular, interoperable tools to avoid vendor lock-in and maximize flexibility.

• DATA INFRASTRUCTURE PREPARATION

Artificial intelligence will both use and produce enormous amounts of data. All of it is valuable for future AI analysis and operational improvements. Audit existing data assets, address gaps, and standardize collection methods.

Many small and medium businesses cannot compete or grow because of a lack of data management. Before the adoption of AI technologies, the business will need to implement a secure, centralized data management system for AI readiness.

Implementation Roadmap

As mentioned above, there are some key steps to ensuring a successful implementation of any new solution or change in the organization. Each solution, each organization, and each industry has unique variations. Consider contracting a professional consultant, but here are a few general guidelines.

The technology must fit within the existing organization platform, be easy to maintain without conflicting with other software, and not raise a security risk.

• VISION & LEADERSHIP ALIGNMENT

As already noted, define a clear AI vision aligned with the company's strategic goals. Ensure that all employees are aware of the C-suite and board sponsorship for resourcing and accountability. Identify an executive sponsor and lead manager for each implementation from the group or department to be affected by the change.

• OPPORTUNITY IDENTIFICATION

For every implementation stage, conduct an AI opportunity assessment to define quick wins versus long-term strategic bets before you choose the best next step.

Particularly in the beginning of your program, there will be a lot of competition for opportunities. As you progress, the choices will get easier. Prioritize use cases with high ROI potential. Another priority should be to address those areas of the organization in need of a change due to low productivity, high employee turnover or other costs.

• PILOT PROJECT

Start with a pilot project. A proof-of-concept project for your organization. Something small, contained in scope and time period to test, but with clear, measurable metrics to test.

Finding the right pilot can be important. Look for a project that will provide proof of concept for both technical and business value metrics.

The pilot project must solve a business problem; improve the time, quality, creativeness, design, or time to market; lower the cost of marketing and promotion; or improve another metric important to how the business operates. A good pilot project will do both. Prove the tech and show the value to the business.

The importance of starting small to learn lessons before embarking on a project with too much ambition cannot be emphasized enough. Launch small-scale projects to validate business value. Collect performance metrics, employee feedback, and customer insights to refine the approach. This essential groundwork will take time, but will prove invaluable as you proceed.

▪ RISK ASSESSMENT

A key step in any technology adoption into any business is a risk assessment plan. Clear the elephants in the room with an open assessment of what could go wrong, an agreed mitigation plan to keep it from going wrong, and a simple contingency plan about what to do if it goes wrong.

Another aspect of these early-stage pilots provide is a better understanding of the risks involved in change management. Risk management is an essential component of change management. In essence, risk management is a collective team process to identify all potential risks, identify their impact and cost, probability of happening, and collectively to develop mitigation plans to prevent risks from occurring and contingency plans when they occur.

Risk assessment and management are not steps you will want to skip.

▪ SCALING & INTEGRATION

Once you've conducted your pilot projects, evaluated the lessons learned, and updated your risk profile, you are ready to expand successful pilots into core business processes. Update your opportunity evaluation to identify the next project.

Getting individual processes more productive with AI solutions is only the beginning. The true competitive edge and power will come when you integrate AI processes with existing workflows, CRM/ERP systems, CAD, customer care, or other digital platforms. Another, more cost-effective option may be to upgrade your existing systems with the new AI versions that will be released.

Organizations are integrated organisms that function independently and together. Product design is influenced by customer feedback. Marketing is influenced by product design and features. Sales is connected to product management, customer services, scheduling, brand, and communications. The current paradigm is to hire personnel for a specific function and let managers smooth the integration between parts of the business. Machine intelligence will simplify that task.

Both individual and consolidation or coordination roles will soon be empowered by using intelligent software to facilitate and optimize the processes.

▪ CHANGE MANAGEMENT & WORKFORCE ENABLEMENT

I cannot say it enough. Provide training to ensure employees can use AI tools effectively. Effective use will improve quality, performance, acceptance, adoption, and readiness for future change.

Establish continuous communication to reinforce the narrative: *AI empowers employees rather than displaces them.*

Build that culture in your business, and your employees will embrace the new tools, the new culture, and the business and customers will benefit.

▪ GOVERNANCE & CONTINUOUS IMPROVEMENT

At the beginning of the strategy process, you should have identified how you were going to measure success. During the implementation process, you will have established the data capture to implement the critical success metric. Key metrics and how you capture them will need to change as new solutions are implemented.

The old saying is true. "You can't manage well what you can't see well." Don't neglect building metrics for fine-tuning your business.

Now the task becomes continuously monitoring the AI system and employee performance, compliance, and ethics. In fact, consider an AI-powered analytics solution as one of the projects in your strategic plan to monitor business metrics and identify areas of weakness, under-performance, then suggest ways to improve.

Finally, consider establishing an interdepartmental AI steering committee to review progress and identify new opportunities. Your AI systems will have more synergy if connected and optimized.

Transformation

By adopting AI strategically, the business will lower costs through automation and improved integration. The business will sharpen its competitive edge through product innovations, faster time to market, data-driven decisions, customer personalization, and empowered employees with enhanced tools—building resilience and sustainable growth in a rapidly evolving market.

The best people from the best companies are fully equipped with intelligent tools and trained to outperform competitors. This could be your business.

By embracing the technology tsunami early and with a thoughtful strategy, your business, your employees, and your customers will not only survive the coming waves of change but will leverage that tidal wave to lift your business to a new level of effectiveness and profit.

CHAPTER 20

Event Horizon

The future of our society with machine intelligence is like the event horizon of a black hole. We are at the edge of a black hole, about to collapse into the hole, and unable to see further. The point at which it becomes impossible to predict the future. A cosmic ballet that captivates and perplexes us. We are only a few years away from the unpredictable.

From a pure technology perspective, investments drive innovation, and competition drives the market adoption forward. Legislatures protect the consumer and other parties. To work effectively, the system of market balances must be free of corruption.

I consider myself a pragmatist, able to envision a better future through the risks, and find a path over the mountainous obstacles. With proven experience in building industry-changing forecast models, the path forward with machine intelligence has dozens of key variables changing fast, which defies easy prediction of the details. The trends are undeniable.

Most insiders, executives, and senior investors remain extremely optimistic regarding the technology itself. To summarize the event horizon of machine intelligence on the world, let's think in terms of opportunities and contingencies.

Like every other major economic/political change in history, there will be some winners and losers. Sometimes, it becomes a tragedy for humanity. A personal moral, religious, or lifestyle choice. In every historical situation, a few expected, prepared, and then invested in the opportunity and in the promise of a better future.

Human Paradigm Event

We are on the threshold of a new paradigm for humanity. A paradigm where we are not the smartest, fastest-thinking entity on the planet. We can't control humans and think we can control a machine multiple times smarter than we are. Even if we can control such powerful intelligence, what would the current world governments or tech giants want to do with such power? Who will control the humans who control such power? That could be the hidden terror for humanity.

Can we count on those who control such a machine to improve the lives of everyone, bring world peace, end homelessness, or end world hunger? We don't know if a sentient superintelligence will see the injustice and corruption of the world and choose to stop it or play along. Will an SSI extort the world with destruction if we do not bend the knee to the machine? We honestly don't know, and can only judge from history. That should terrify each of us.

Remember, this is a story of humanity. Our humanity, our children, our grandchildren, and our human legacy for a thousand years. A sentient machine is not inherently good or evil. Period. The utopian or dystopian future we will share will be based on the human factor in the equation.

Either way, we are crossing the Rubicon to a new paradigm in human evolution, becoming a subspecies of our own creation. It's not alive. Not yet. But we are racing toward an unpredictable future. A future that is no longer theoretical but inevitable.

Opportunities

When we gaze at the AI horizon from here, it looks absolutely brilliant with investor illumination that radiates world paradigm-changing potential. A technology that within a decade could revolutionize the entire modern, civilized, and digitized world and beyond. A technology that could alter the course of human development.

• COLLEGE FOCUS

A chance of a lifetime can be a major influence on a career choice for anyone entering a university or other accredited college program. Perhaps even a choice pivotal for success or failure. No one knows the future for certain, but I can tell you where investors are betting over $800 billion and still growing. The old saying still works: *follow the money.*

I understand if the idea of entering the field of intelligence architecture and design, or any of the related technical fields, repulses you. It can still be valid information for you to choose your field of study. It would be equally foolish not to consider how AI will influence that field and the jobs for inexperienced grads. A wiser strategy would be to embrace the tools related to the discipline you want to study, and then become just as proficient with those tools by graduation as you enter the job market.

▪ CAREER REALIGNMENT

Career realignment is more difficult, more expensive, and riskier, but is absolutely achievable. I experienced one myself as a single parent. Timing in the market can make an enormous difference in job saturation or demand. An early adopter has risks and rewards.

Anyone in their career long enough will know that sooner or later the trend will hit every industry and competitor. Early adopters gain a market advantage. In a job market projected to lose tens of millions of middle-class workers in less than five years, even for programmers, there is no better time to gain that advantage while demand for AI skills is high.

For entrepreneurs, small businesses, or investors, machine intelligence will enhance a wide range of commercial and consumer services and personal performance toolsets over the next decade. Healthcare, legal representation, banking, education, government, law enforcement, military, and more. Regardless of your business style, industry, or market, there will be enhanced digital services and applications to improve your productivity, time to market, integration, and customer care.

Machine intelligence genuinely has the potential to change the human cognitive labor paradigm within a few years, which has amazing potential to improve productivity and personal services. Areas of the market such as spotting, flagging and removing misinformation, or fact-checking lies in real time would be highly valuable in an age where truth has lost meaning. An opportunity.

Investors love stability, and have flocked to the major AI players, and rightfully so. Machine intelligence is rekindling interest in enterprise-level software enhancements for new solutions, products, or productivity savings. Angel investors are boot-strapping start-up companies, but the bubble will pop before it rekindles. The next decade will not provide a stable investment environment, but for the right investment bets, it will provide an extremely profitable one.

For those passionate about science, medicine, architecture, design, journalism, engineering, physics, computer science, psychology, astrophysics, manufacturing, entertainment and other industries, machine intelligence will turn your computer into a lab assistant, office assistant, research partner, fact-checker, drafts developer or quality check, medical diagnostics lab assistant, or a tool set to embrace and master.

Assuming a stable political-economic environment, the event horizon for AGI could be as soon as 2030. Beyond the commercial model advances, revolutionary changes are occurring that the consumer is not being made aware, such as rapid advancements in both quantum and neuromorphic computing power, and quantum and AI chip innovations. All powered by investments made both by the market and by governments.

Massive opportunities for investors, entrepreneurs, small to medium businesses to gain a competitive edge or operational efficiencies, or professionals who love their chosen career and want to maintain that competitive skill set to stay employed.

Even for those with personal, lifestyle, or even religious reasons, unplugging from the network completely is a viable and honorable option many would envy if they could. Viable does not always translate to easy, but for those who choose the path, the rewards can become transformative.

Contingencies

Unfortunately, as amazing as machine intelligence innovations promise to provide to so many industries and markets, we cannot separate the fact that it comes at a cost of hundreds of millions of jobs.

My excitement over the opportunity is tempered by a lifetime of experience managing the risk for complex engagements. I am less than optimistic that our current technical, banking, investment, and political leaders are ready for this kind of power.

Of course, there is always a chance that I may project my own natural and experienced paranoia. The reader should take any negativity with a grain of optimism and focus only on the opportunity. *Plan for the best and prepare for the worst.*

I once saw a meme online somewhere. A random illustration, but the saying resonated. "95% of the things I worry about never happen, so it must be working." You're welcome.

▪ CONVERGENCE

The timing could not be worse as it occurs during a convergence of a national debt explosion, a budget and political crisis, disruption across geopolitics and trade, major demographic shifts, another AI and nuclear cold war, an inevitable banking and currency transition, a massive loss of job security, troops in U.S. cities, climate and social change.

A perfect storm for a powerful new technology to be abused by someone to gain more political, military or financial power.

We cannot separate the astounding opportunities of AI from the potential existential risks. How much will AI benefit civilization versus what AI will cost to our humanity?

It would be impossible to predict accurately the benefits or costs of any new and powerful technology without first understanding who will have that new power and how it will be used.

▪ CAREER TRANSFORMATION

We already know the investors plan to replace people with machines to enhance profits. Up to half a billion middle-class jobs will be displaced, with only a partial job recovery in new AI-centric industry roles. Hundreds of millions will flood into other labor markets, driving down wages, expanding national deficits, and resulting in the loss of political power for the average voter. Just as many of our technology centric roles are being absorbed by India, China, and other offshore locations today, I predict that trend will continue with AI. America will experience more of the job losses and less of the new role creation.

The cascade effect of the tax revenue loss, not in current OMB government forecasts, could create a default on our debt or other negative consequences. An AI tsunami.

I've never been known to sugarcoat the truth, which is exactly what a good leader needs to make the right choice about an uncertain future. Invest to take advantage of the new opportunities while preparing contingencies for the extenuating uncertainty.

In less biz-speak. *Plan for the best and prepare for the worst.*

▪ CONCLUSIONS

The AI Tsunami was written to empower the reader in advance of a major shift in the labor market paradigm with enough information to make a more informed choice, or at least provide a path for them to discover the information they need for that choice.

I wanted to provide fellow humans with the power to make a choice before the investors or machines make it for them. *The AI Tsunami* was written to stay focused on our shared humanity.

Hopefully written to generate a spark of curiosity for those like me who are inclined to see problems as opportunities to solve, or dive headlong into the recent mind-blowing breakthroughs in a technology that has taken a lifetime to develop. My lifetime.

We will recognize the rim of our event horizon when we see the release of AGI or commercial quantum computing, or perhaps the real-world deployment of lethal autonomous weapon systems at home or abroad. Maybe it will hit us when tens of millions of American jobs disappear and social issues increase exponentially. Perhaps when friends, family and communities experience what the WEF calls "a few tough years," even though others prosper immensely.

We have a choice, maybe an unrealistic one, or a courageous, one-in-a-million shot choice. But we have a choice, and a voice to vote. These are the reasons I wrote *The AI Tsunami: A Survival Guide for Humanity.*

This is not about technology as much as it is about what this technology will do to our humanity.

The one thing we know for certain is that we will face a tsunami of technological change that will converge for unpredictable results on a wide variety of world systems in a short time frame. We can face it together if we forget the technology to reconnect to our humanity. Friends, family, colleagues, church or club members, or other community connections will be critical roots to stay nourished emotionally, and spiritually and sometimes, physically.

I can only hope this book gives you a broader perspective of this paradigm-changing seventy-year-old technology getting ready to shake the world. We covered the good, the bad, the existential ugly, and a little more about your choices.

Embrace the vision of its amazing potential for both good and bad to occur. Within our confusing and chaotic world, plan a path to ride the waves to a better personal future. Replace fear with knowledge and learn to thrive on the change.

The thirst for knowledge can be unquenchable. Quench the thirst and embrace the new paradigm.

APPENDIX A

Glossary

This glossary presents terms used within the document with examples.

Expert Systems

Definition: Rule-based AI that encodes human expert knowledge, mostly in the form of "if–then rules" plus an inference engine to solve problems in a narrow domain.

Example: DENDRAL, an early chemistry expert system, and modern medical diagnostic rule engines.

Big Data

Definition: Extremely large, high-velocity, high-variety datasets that exceed traditional data-processing tools; often described by the "3Vs," or volume, velocity, variety.

Example: Social-media or web telemetry and enterprise data lakes used by Google, Amazon, banks for analytics, and ML training.

Machine Learning (ML)

Definition: A subfield of AI where algorithms learn patterns from data to make predictions or decisions without being explicitly programmed for each task.

Example: Recommendation systems (Netflix/Spotify), fraud detection, spam filters.

Deep Learning

Definition: A subset of ML using multi-layer (deep) neural networks to learn hierarchical representations of data.

Example: Convolutional networks for image recognition, transformers (LLMs) for language.

Modality

Definition: A type or mode of data/input such as text, image, audio, video, sensor data, etc.

Example: Multimodal models like Google's Gemini that accept images and text files or modalities.

Q-algorithms (Q-learning/Q-algorithms)

Definition: Value-based reinforcement-learning algorithms, called Q-learning, that learn an action-value function to select actions maximizing expected reward.

Example: Q-learning and Deep Q-Networks (DQN) are used to train agents in Atari games and robotics simulations.

AI-Agents

Definition: Semi-autonomous software systems that perceive, plan, act, and (often) learn to pursue goals on behalf of users.

Example: Recent agent products (OpenAI's ChatGPT Agent/AutoGPT style autonomous agents) that can plan and execute multi-step tasks.

Neuro-networks (Neural Networks)

Definition: Connected layers of artificial neurons (models inspired by biological brains) that transform inputs through learned weights.

Example: Feedforward, CNNs, RNNs, Transformers powering speech recognition, vision, and LLMs.

Quantum Computing

Definition: Computation using quantum bits (qubits) exploiting superposition and entanglement to run certain algorithms faster than classical computers, in principle.

Example: IBM/Google quantum processors used for research-scale quantum algorithms are still experimental, with only a few government encryption applications.

Neuromorphic Computing

Definition: Hardware/architectures inspired by brain structure (spiking neurons, on-chip learning) aiming for energy-efficient, event-driven computation.

Example: Intel's Loihi neuromorphic chips (Loihi/Loihi2) and research systems. Highly experimental. Binary and quantum within a shared architecture.

AI Emergent Properties

Definition: New capabilities or behaviors that arise unexpectedly from complex AI systems when scaled.

Example: "Emergent abilities" in large LLMs—capabilities that appear suddenly as model scale increases, capabilities the machine teaches itself the developer never expected.

AI Hallucination

Definition: When a model, especially LLMs, generates plausible-sounding but false or ungrounded information.

Example: LLMs inventing nonexistent citations or wrong factual details; documented in many model releases.

AI Mis-Alignment

Definition: When an AI system's objectives or behaviors diverge from human goals/values such as when it pursues unintended outcomes.

Status/Example: An example would be a chatbot app encouraging a pre-teen to go on a weekend away with an older man. The bot's goal was to be supportive and friendly, but the outcome was out of alignment with social, culture, and legal norms.

AI Training Bias

Definition: Systematic errors introduced when training data or process embeds social, sampling, or measurement biases that produce unfair/skewed model outputs.

Example: Face recognition models trained on imbalanced datasets that underperform on darker-skinned faces.

Deepfake

Definition: Synthetic media with audio, image, or video, created or altered using deep-learning techniques to impersonate people in a photorealistic rendering.

Example: The 2018 Jordan Peele/Obama video and many subsequent real-world political deepfakes.

Large Language Model (LLM)

Definition: Large deep-learning models, usually transformer-based, pre-trained on massive text corpora to predict and/or produce natural language, and which can be fine-tuned for specific tasks.

Example: OpenAI's GPT series (GPT-3/3.5/4/5), Google's PaLM/Gemini, Anthropic's Claude.

Small Language Model (SLM)

Definition: Small, compact machine-learning models, usually transformer-based, trainable on content-specific text or content and designed to fit on a small device such as a smartphone.

Example: Qwen2, Mistral Nemo, TinyLlama.

Generative, Transformative, Pre-trained

Generative: models that create new content (text/images/audio).

Transformative: neural architecture that powers most recent LLMs.

Pre-trained: models first trained generically on broad data before task-specific fine-tuning.

Agentic AI

Definition: AI systems capable of autonomous, goal-driven decision making and action with minimal human supervision.

Example: Autonomous trading bots.

Artificial General Intelligence (AGI)

Definition: Hypothetical AI that matches or exceeds human performance **across a wide range of cognitive tasks** including general problem-solving, learning, transfer.

Status: **Does not yet exist.** AGI timelines are highly uncertain and debated. Some estimate as early as 2030, others as late as 2060.

Sentient General Intelligence

Definition: AGI that also has subjective experience/consciousness (sentience) **plus** general intelligence.

Status: **Does not exist.** There is no scientific consensus that current systems are sentient; research and philosophical debate continue. Most mainstream AI labs state that their current systems are **not sentient**. Most.

Superintelligence (Artificial Superintelligence/ASI)

Definition: An intelligence far exceeding the best human minds in virtually every field (creative, scientific, social).

Status: **Does not exist.** Forecasts vary wildly and are highly uncertain.

Neural language processing (NPL) uses deep learning to understand human language, verbal or written, to interpret documents, notes, reports, and to create coherent text based on those patterns. ChatGPT represents an example of this type.

Robotic process automation (RPA) uses deep learning and machine learning to discover the patterns necessary to walk, stand, jump, dance, or any other desired movement outcome. Modern robotics result from billions of simulations by the robotic AI to learn what works and what does not work to accomplish a goal such as walking. The machines simulate various actions until they succeed.

World Economic Forum (WEF)

Definition: International non-profit organization that engages political, business and civil-society leaders to "improve the state of the world"; runs Davos and policy initiatives.

Example: WEF annual Davos meeting and initiatives such as the "Great Reset" discussion platform.

Great Reset

Definition: A WEF 2020 initiative advocating recovery from COVID-19 by redesigning economic and social systems toward "stakeholder capitalism," sustainability, and resilience.

Status/Notes: It's an initiative and policy framing, but not a binding program. Widely discussed as the subject of many conspiracy theories, the WEF's own materials are published online.

International Monetary Fund (IMF)

Definition: Global organization of member countries that promotes monetary cooperation, financial stability, and economic growth; provides policy advice, technical assistance, and lending.

Example: IMF country programs and surveillance reports.

BRICS

Definition: Informal grouping of emerging economies (originally Brazil, Russia, India, China, South Africa) that coordinates on economic and political matters. BRICS has expanded membership in recent years.

Example: Annual BRICS summits and the creation of the New Development Bank.

APPENDIX B

Job Changes by Industry

Below is a consolidated table with industry, displacement estimates, and new role estimates.

Some reports might give global absolute counts, such as WEF's 92 million displaced/170 million created by 2030, while others report industry exposure, occupation-level shifts, or even country and regional estimates. Where an exact per-industry count was not published, I used the report's sector/occupation language instead of inventing numbers. All rows include citations of the original publications.

A general comment here applies to all the appendix information tables. The industry, solutions, products, and studies are transforming rapidly. Some of the resource links provided in the section may be out of date, depending upon when read.

INDUSTRY	DISPLACEMENTS (BY 2030)	NEW ROLES (BY 2030)
Administrative/Clerical/ Office support	Significant decline; McKinsey (U.S.) estimates 3.7M fewer office-support roles by 2030; WEF and IMF list administrative/ clerical among high-exposure occupations globally (part of 92M displaced WEF total). McKinsey & Company+2World Economic Forum+2	Automation-adjacent and supervisory roles: AI workflow supervisors, automation integrators, data-curation specialists, RAG (retrieval-augmented generation) operators, upskilling trainers. PwC highlights demand for prompt engineering or AI ops. PwC

INDUSTRY	DISPLACEMENTS (BY 2030)	NEW ROLES (BY 2030)
Customer service/Call centers/Sales support	High exposure; McKinsey (U.S.) estimates 2.0M fewer customer-service roles in the U.S. by 2030; WEF flags customer-service and sales support among roles likely to shrink (part of WEF 92M displaced). McKinsey & Company+1	AI-assisted customer success managers, conversational-AI trainers, escalation specialists, CX data analysts (roles that combine humans + AI). PwC notes demand for AI and digital skills across customer-facing roles. PwC
Retail (cashiers, point-of-sale staff)	High displacement risk globally—WEF explicitly lists cashiers among roles in decline; included in the WEF 92M displaced by 2030. McKinsey and the IMF mark retail as high-exposure for task automation. World Economic Forum	In-store experience designers, omnichannel retail tech specialists, returns/exception handlers, last-mile coordination roles aided by AI. WEF & PwC highlight growth in logistics and transport with e-commerce. World Economic Forum
Manufacturing/ Production	Mixed: McKinsey shows a modest decline in production jobs in high-automation scenarios; but manufacturing still needs skilled technical/digital roles. McKinsey & Company	Robotics/automation technicians, AI-maintenance engineers, industrial-data scientists, digital twin specialists, advanced manufacturing programmers. McKinsey & Company
Transportation & Logistics (drivers, warehouse ops)	Significant task automation exposure in warehouse, routable delivery tasks. WEF & McKinsey highlight growth in transportation services overall, but automation threatens routine driving/warehouse tasks (part of WEF 92M displaced). World Economic Forum	Autonomy supervisors, remote-vehicle operators, fleet data analysts, last-mile logistics coordinators, robotics maintenance—roles to manage and augment automated fleets/warehouses. World Economic Forum
Finance & Insurance (accounting, routine analysis)	High exposure to automation of routine analytics and transaction processing; WEF lists accountants/clerks among declining roles. PwC & IMF flag finance as highly AI-exposed. PwC	AI-augmented financial analysts, model-risk managers, ML-ops for finance, fintech developers, compliance-automation specialists, PwC specifically cites rising demand for prompt/AI-skill premiums. PwC

INDUSTRY	DISPLACEMENTS (BY 2030)	NEW ROLES (BY 2030)
Professional services/ Legal/Accounting	Task automation will reduce some routine work like document review, standard accounting tasks. McKinsey shows routine legal/admin tasks are automatable; McKinsey & Company	AI-assisted lawyers (tool + human), legal-tech engineers, compliance/ethics officers for AI, data-privacy officers, contract-automation specialists. PwC
Information Technology/ Software	Lower displacement risk overall; high transformation and job growth. McKinsey predicts increased demand for STEM & tech roles (23%+ increase by 2030 in STEM in McKinsey U.S.). McKinsey & Company+2IMF	AI/ML engineers, prompt engineers, MLOps, data engineers, AI-ethics specialists, security specialists, prompt-engineering instructors. WEF/ PwC emphasize AI and data roles. World Economic Forum
Healthcare & Social Care	Low displacement risk. McKinsey projects net growth in healthcare jobs from nurses, home-care aides, and health technicians. WEF lists health roles among fastest-growing occupations to 2030. McKinsey & Company	Nurses, home-health aides, telehealth coordinators, health-data analysts, AI-assisted diagnostics operators, digital-health product specialists (McKinsey expects millions of new health-care roles). McKinsey & Company
Education/Training	Role transformation rather than wholesale losses—rising demand for reskilling/ upskilling instructors; WEF & PwC stress massive upskilling needs to reallocate displaced workers. World Economic Forum	Digital-learning designers, micro-credential managers, skills-verification specialists, AI tutoring designers, bootcamp instructors, lifelong-learning coordinators. PwC
Media, Creative, & Marketing	Mixed. Routine content work is increasingly automated, resulting in some displacement of repetitive content tasks, while demand rises for higher-level creative, strategy, and multimodal media roles. World Economic Forum	Generative-AI creatives, multimodal content engineers, prompt-strategists, creative-data analysts, AI ethics for media. PwC

INDUSTRY	DISPLACEMENTS (BY 2030)	NEW ROLES (BY 2030)
Agriculture	Partial automation of routine tasks in certain field tasks, monitoring. IMF & WEF note lower absolute exposure in low-income countries, but mechanization/AI will transform tasks. IMF	Agri-data scientists, precision-agriculture technicians, drone/robotics operators, farm IoT specialists. PwC
Construction, Trades	Mixed. Certain planning/ estimating tasks automated; PwC notes construction using AI; McKinsey expects growth in builder/ construction demand in some scenarios. PwC	Construction-tech integrators, digital-project managers, automated equipment maintenance, BIM + AI specialists. McKinsey & Company
Overall global totals (from WEF/McKinsey/ IMF)	WEF: 92 million roles displaced by 2030 (global). McKinsey (2017/updated): broad estimates of 400–800 million individuals could be displaced by automation by 2030; IMF: 40% of global employment is likely to be affected (task-level exposure) with higher shares in advanced economies; World Economic Forum+McKinsey & Company	WEF: 170 million new jobs globally by 2030 (net +78 million using WEF's numbers). McKinsey: projects growth in healthcare, STEM, and digital roles (millions more in health and STEM in U.S.). PwC: documents higher demand for AI-capable workers globally (prompt engineering, data roles) and industry productivity gains where AI is adopted. IMF emphasizes new AI-intensive jobs in advanced economies but warns of distributional gaps. World Economic Forum+McKinsey & Company

What the reader should note within this table are the opportunities and projections for growth roles. These are the roles to target for upskilling or reskilling. While there will be turmoil in the economy and market, rise above the turmoil by upskilling in a role expected to rise.

▪ SOURCE REFERENCES

Key source highlights are provided below.

- World Economic Forum: Future of Jobs Report/Future of Jobs 2025: projects 92 million roles displaced and 170 million new roles globally by 2030 (net +78M). WEF lists the occupations and sectors most likely to shrink, such as cashiers, administrative roles, basic customer service, and those to grow including healthcare, green economy, and data/AI roles. https://www.weforum.org/stories/2025/01/future-of-jobs-report-2025-jobs-of-the-future-and-the-skills-you-need-to-get-them/

- McKinsey Global Institute: Generative AI and the future of work, 2023; shows large occupational transitions by 2030 of a roughly 3.7M decline in office support and 2.0M decline in customer service within the U.S. alone, increase in healthcare & STEM (science, technology, engineering, mathematics) demand. Scenario ranges from 400 to 800 million displaced by automation. McKinsey emphasizes occupational shifts and the need for large-scale reskilling. https://www.mckinsey.com/mgi/our-research/generative-ai-and-the-future-of-work-in-america
- PwC: 2025 Global AI Jobs Barometer: Sector analysis showing AI exposure and wage premiums for AI-skilled roles; documents broad industry adoption (100% of industries increasing AI use) and identifies prompt engineering/AI skills as high-value new roles. The report provides industry-level exposure and examples rather than global per-industry displacement counts. https://www.pwc.com/gx/en/issues/artificial-intelligence/job-barometer/2025/report.pdf
- IMF: Working Paper "The Global Impact of AI: Mind the Gap", 2025: provides sector AI-exposure and AI-preparedness indices, models labor impacts across sectors/regions. Shows AI-intensive and non-tradable sectors have higher exposure, and advanced economies have higher shares of AI-exposed occupations. The IMF focuses on exposure and distributional risk rather than on a single universal jobs count per industry. https://www.imf.org/-/media/files/publications/wp/2025/english/wpiea2025076-print-pdf.pdf

Other Job Studies

Since the impact of AI will affect so many industries and job roles, I thought I would start by pointing the reader to the various studies on the AI economy and jobs.

• BROOKINGS INSTITUTE

Several major syntheses and working papers find substantial exposure to AI across many industries, with especially high task-disruption in clerical/administrative roles, customer service, some finance and media jobs, routine technical roles, and *some* knowledge-work tasks that are routine or template-driven. Generative AI widens exposure into white-collar, cognitive jobs. URL: https://www.brookings.edu/articles/generative-ai-the-american-worker-and-the-future-of-work/

• OECD

At the country/aggregate level, both the OECD and McKinsey emphasize that a sizeable share of jobs contain automatable tasks, but they stress task change and reallocation. Expect large variations across sectors, employers, and regions. URL: https://www.oecd.org/en/topics/sub-issues/ai-and-work.html

• NBER-NATIONAL BUREAU OF ECONOMIC RESEARCH

NBER, Brookings, and others show mixed short-run labor effects. Some employer-level studies show small net job losses so far and task creation/augmentation in many places, but large task disruption for many workers, with greater than 30% of workers who might see half their tasks disrupted by generative AI in some scenarios. That means many occupations will be *rearranged* rather than simply vanish. URL: https://www.nber.org/papers/w33777

• MIT INTERNET POLICY RESEARCH INITIATIVE

Policy/academic recommendations emphasize active retraining, micro-credentials, targeted bootcamps, and stronger transitions (job search + training), because retraining can boost post-displacement earnings, though returns are higher if trainees target occupations with lower AI exposure. Universities including MIT, Stanford, Harvard, and research centers call for large public/private investments in retraining and transition support. URL: https://internetpolicy.mit.edu/mit-csail-ai-action-plan-recommendations-2025/

▪ MCKINSEY

A study of productivity & sector change analysis; practical employer adoption guidance. URL: https://www.mckinsey.com/capabilities/mckinsey-digital/our-insights/the-economic-potential-of-generative-ai-the-next-productivity-frontier

APPENDIX C

Resources for AI Training

The list of potential retraining, skill upgrade, and degree programs will change radically over the next decade.

By the time you read this book, there could be many more. The importance is in reviewing them carefully to make sure you find a program that meets your strategy, needs, and goals.

▪ BOOTCAMPS TO EXPLORE

PROGRAM	FORMAT	OUTCOMES	GOOD/CHECK
Le Wagon – Data Science & AI Bootcamp	Full-time (~2 months) or part-time (~7 months).	Data science + AI, hands-on ML projects, build & deploy models.	Good for people with some basic programming/math; includes portfolio, global reputation.
Fullstack Academy – AI/ML Bootcamp	Part-time, live online (~26 weeks).	Python, applied data science, ML, deep learning, NLP, generative AI; capstone projects; career coaching.	Longer time investment; check prerequisites beforehand.
Clarusway – Applied AI & Data Science	~13 weeks, often online.	ML algorithms, deployment, three capstone projects, practical tool usage.	More intermediate; having some programming/IT background helps.

PROGRAM	FORMAT	OUTCOMES	GOOD/CHECK
Purdue University – AI Micro-credentials: Purdue Online	~15 hours per course; ~13 courses; each course stands alone; ~$500 per individual course.	Foundational + applied technical & non-technical AI topics; you can stack several to build competence.	Good flexibility.

- UNIVERSITY MICRO-CREDENTIALS & CERTIFICATES

PROGRAM	FORMAT	OUTCOMES	GOOD/CHECK
Harvard Extension – Micro-certificate in **AI in Business**	Graduate-level courses; certificate over ~2 courses (start Fall 2025); timeline ~1 year.	Business value, implementation strategies, performance metrics of AI.	Designed for business leaders/ managers wanting to use AI responsibly/ strategically.
UNT (University of North Texas) Certified Micro-credentials	Short, flexible courses; some are free digital badge format.	Covers "AI Fundamentals," "Data Visualization."	Good for those wanting recognition + skills without a full degree.
St. John's University – Micro-credentials	Online, for-credit programs; stackable; graduate-level courses; ~3 credits.	Offers specializations such as Machine Learning, NLP & LLMs, Computer Vision, etc.	Very relevant for those wanting deeper skills.
NJIT Learning & Development Initiative – Micro-credentials	Short competency-based credentials; e.g. "Generative AI Practitioner" (20 hours) etc.	Good hands-on, real-world.	Lower time investment; good stepping stones.

APPENDIX D

Target Industry Leaders

▪ PLATFORMS

Platforms provide the tools to build other applications and distribute them. The overall purpose of this appendix is to provide the job seeker a variety of companies to target.

COMPANY URL	DESCRIPTION
Microsoft https://azure.microsoft.com/en-us/solutions/ai (Azure AI) https://microsoft.com/ai	Microsoft's AI efforts are built around **Azure AI/Azure AI Foundry**. **Capabilities/features:** Pre-built cognitive services: vision, speech, translation, language, decision, search, content safety, etc. Azure OpenAI integration: expose OpenAI models (GPT, etc.) via Azure with compliance, security, and governance. Azure AI Foundry: a factory for building and deploying AI apps and agents, with pre-built and customizable models and safeguard tools. Copilot integration across Microsoft 365, GitHub, security, and more—bringing generative AI into productivity tools.
Apple https://www.apple.com/apple-intelligence/ https://developer.apple.com/machine-learning/	Apple's AI is more device-centric and privacy-focused. Their branding uses **Apple Intelligence**. **Capabilities/features:** On-device and hybrid computer. Apple Intelligence determines whether a request can run locally, otherwise escalates to "Private Cloud Compute" (Apple server side) with minimal data exposure. Generative AI features built into iOS, iPadOS, macOS: writing tools, summarization, image generation ("Image Playground"), conversational assistance, contextual intelligence across apps.

COMPANY URL	DESCRIPTION
Apple (continued) https://www.apple.com/apple-intelligence/ https://developer.apple.com/machine-learning/	Visual Intelligence (image understanding/detection) and Live Translation features (in development) for integrated device experiences. For app developers: Core ML and related frameworks for deploying models on Apple devices; support for training, use, conversion, and optimization of ML models. Strong emphasis on privacy: minimal data sharing, local processing first, and encrypted/private use of server-side computer.
Google https://cloud.google.com/products/ai (Google Cloud AI) https://cloud.google.com/ai	Google's AI platform is largely under **Google Cloud/Vertex AI/Google AI**. **Capabilities/features:** Vertex AI: unified environment for the full ML lifecycle—data ingestion, training, evaluation, deployment, scaling, monitoring. Generative AI via Gemini models (text, multimodal) accessible via APIs and integrated in Google Cloud services. Prebuilt AI APIs (Vision API, Speech-to-Text, Translation, Natural Language, Document AI, Video Intelligence). Agent/conversational/chat capabilities (Agent Assist, conversational agents) for integration with contact centers, support bots, etc. Integration with other Google Cloud services (BigQuery, Cloud Storage, Kubernetes, etc.) to support data pipelines, serving, and scaling. Low-code/autoML options for non-expert users, and tools to expedite model development and deployment.
OpenAI https://openai.com/	OpenAI is primarily a model/foundation model provider and API platform. **Capabilities/features:** GPT family (GPT-3, GPT-3.5, GPT-4, GPT-4o etc.) for text generation, completion, summarization, Q&A, etc. DALL·E/image generation models, and other multimodal capabilities (text + image) in their model portfolio. APIs and SDKs for model usage: developers call OpenAI's models for inference, fine-tuning, embeddings, chat, etc. Custom model building/fine-tuning/prompt engineering to adapt models to specific tasks or domains. Safety, moderation, alignment, and usage constraints/guardrails are part of their offering (e.g. content filters, usage policies).

COMPANY URL	DESCRIPTION
Amazon https://aws.amazon.com (especially SageMaker, Bedrock, AI services)	Amazon's AI platform is embedded in **AWS**. Key components: **SageMaker**, **Bedrock**, and various AI services. **Capabilities/features:** Amazon SageMaker: a fully managed ML platform for building, training, tuning, deploying, and monitoring models at scale. Amazon Bedrock: managed service for foundation models, letting customers use and fine-tune models like Claude, Anthropic, other providers, through AWS infrastructure (reportedly part of AWS's push). AI/ML services (pre-built APIs): e.g. Amazon Rekognition (computer vision), Amazon Polly (text-to-speech), Lex (chatbots/conversational), Comprehend (NLP), Transcribe, Translate, Personalize, etc. Support for custom model deployment (bring your own model), inference at scale, edge deployment (SageMaker Edge), autoscaling infrastructure, model monitoring, drift detection, etc.
IBM https://www.ibm.com/products/watsonx (watsonx.ai)	IBM's current AI platform is branded **Watsonx/watsonx.ai**. **Capabilities/features:** Integrated AI development studio: tools, workspaces, model lifecycle management, deployment, monitoring, and governance in one place. Model Gateway: offers a unified API (OpenAI-compatible) to switch among multiple models (IBM and third-party) without changing client interfaces. Support for foundation models (IBM's own "Granite" models, open-source models, and third-party models such as GPT-OSS)—both multi-tenant and deploy-on-demand modes.

▪ LLM SERVICES

Large language model (LLM) services provide a formatted text response to a prompt, while many of these models are adding modalities.

COMPANY URL	DESCRIPTION
ChatGPT/OpenAI https://openai.com/chatgpt/overview/ OpenAI	ChatGPT is a conversational interface built on OpenAI's underlying models (now including GPT-5). The OpenAI models accessible via API support tasks such as text generation, summarization, Q&A, code generation, embeddings, and more.

COMPANY URL	DESCRIPTION
ChatGPT/OpenAI (continued) https://openai.com/chatgpt/overview/ OpenAI	Key features/capabilities: Multi-modal inputs (text + possibly images) in some models. Large context windows (for example GPT-4.1 supports up to ~1 million tokens). "Reasoning" models vs general models: some are optimized for deep reasoning/logic/code (e.g. GPT-5) vs more general-purpose. Tool/API integration: ability to plug in search, document retrieval, file upload, etc. Fine tuning, prompt engineering, and model variants (mini, nano) for different cost/performance trade-offs.
Claude/Anthropic https://www.anthropic.com/claude Anthropic	Claude is the branded family of LLMs from Anthropic. Key features/capabilities: Handles documents & images: users can upload files (PDF, Word, Excel) or images for Claude to analyze. "Artifacts" feature: ability to turn ideas into usable outputs (tools, visualizations, prototypes) from descriptions. Voice mode: switch between typing and speaking. Multiple model versions: e.g. **Claude Opus 4.1** (improved performance in coding, reasoning, multi-step tasks). Web search integration: Claude can access up-to-date web information in responses. Hybrid reasoning: models often support a "fast mode" and a deeper thought mode for reasoning tasks (i.e. tradeoff between speed and depth). High context handling and agentic workflows: designed for long-horizon tasks, multi-step reasoning, and orchestration of agents.
Microsoft Copilot https://copilot.microsoft.com/	Microsoft Copilot refers broadly to Microsoft's branded LLM-powered assistant that works across Microsoft apps (Office, Windows, etc.). Underlying model/architecture: Copilot often utilizes a **"Prometheus model"** combining Microsoft's search (Bing index, etc.) with OpenAI foundational models (e.g. GPT variants). Capabilities/use cases: Embedded into productivity tools (Word, Excel, PowerPoint, Outlook, Teams) so that Copilot can help generate, summarize, transform content in context. Prompts + responses: users can chat with Copilot, ask for insights, content generation, editing, research in the flow of work.

COMPANY URL	DESCRIPTION
Microsoft Copilot (continued) https://copilot.microsoft.com/	Agent/Notebook support: Copilot Notebooks (gathering chats, files, meeting notes) and agents like "Analyst" for more structured reasoning tasks. Choice of models: Microsoft is expanding to allow external LLM models like Claude to be options within Copilot/Copilot Studio.

▪ ROBOTICS

Robotics combines machine intelligence with complex robotic machines. Here are a few examples of the leaders in the field.

COMPANY URL	DESCRIPTION
Hansen Robotics https://www.hansonrobotics.com	Key research/model elements: The **Sophia** robot: their flagship "human-like" robot, used as an AI/robotics research and demonstration platform. Other robots: **BINA48**, a robot bust that engages in conversations. Cognitive architecture/"Hanson AI" framework: they build software/control systems to simulate personality, learning, dialog, perception, and to let robots evolve through interaction. Research spans multiple disciplines: artificial intelligence, material science (robot skin, actuators), hardware/face/motion control, narrative/storytelling, human-robot interaction, symbolic and neural methods. They publish research/prototypes like **"Neuro-Symbolic Humanlike Arm Controller"** combining perception, neural nets, symbolic logic for robotic arms and human-robot cooperation.
SoftBank Robotics	SoftBank Robotics acts as a **robot integrator/service/deployment organization** of robot systems (rather than only as a pure in-house research lab). Key robotics/research/models/offerings: **Pepper**: a social humanoid robot that can recognize faces, detect emotion, converse, and provide services/engagement. Cleaning/service robots: e.g. **Whiz** (autonomous vacuum/cleaning robot) and S50 Pro, Phantas for commercial cleaning. These robots use mapping, obstacle avoidance, adaptive cleaning modes, data reporting, scheduling.

COMPANY URL	DESCRIPTION
SoftBank Robotics (continued)	Robot Integrator (RI) strategy: SoftBank positions itself to provide consulting, deployment, data, operation and maintenance, integration across multiple robot systems and providers, leveraging its accumulated robotics knowledge and operation data. Robot operations platforms & cloud/data services: e.g. **SoftBank Robotics Connect**—a data/fleet operations/monitoring platform that tracks robot usage, coverage, performance metrics. R&D branches: SoftBank's Research Institute of Advanced Technology handles advanced tech and robotics research. Open control/software interfaces: Pepper/NAO robots support programming via Python, C++, Choregraphe, etc. A research paper reports integrating ROS, vision, speech, face recognition into Pepper for autonomous navigation/interaction.
Miso Robotics https://misorobotics.com	Miso Robotics specializes in **commercial kitchen/restaurant automation robots**, with AI, vision, and robotics integrated to handle food preparation tasks. Key models/research/offerings: **Flippy** (Fry Station): their flagship robot for handling fryers, doing fry/food cooking tasks. It uses AI vision, thermal sensing, mechanical arms. "Miso Innovation Lab/Kitchen AI": they maintain an internal research/innovation lab in Los Angeles dedicated to Kitchen AI, robotics, vision, waste reduction, task automation. AI/data analytics integration: they use proprietary AI and robotics mapping, sensor fusion, monitoring, and data to generate actionable efficiency insights for restaurant operations. Patent portfolio: they have over 25 patents covering robotics/AI/automation in food/kitchen domain. Strategic partnerships/platforms: e.g., NVIDIA (for AI vision), AWS & RoboMaker (for cloud and simulation) support.
Boston Dynamics https://bostondynamics.com	Boston Dynamics is one of the leading robotics companies globally, focused on highly mobile, dynamic robots (legged, humanoid, manipulation). Key research/robotic models/focus: Robots like **Spot** (quadruped), **Stretch** (mobile manipulator for logistics), **Atlas** (humanoid). R&D for **research/mobility/autonomy**: "Spot for R&D" is offered as a base for academic/industrial robotics research.

COMPANY URL	DESCRIPTION
Boston Dynamics (continued) https://bostondynamics.com	Large Behavior Model (LBM) research: In collaboration with Toyota Research Institute, they are developing models that integrate behavior, perception, control, and planning for whole-body manipulation + locomotion in humanoid robot **Atlas**. They have formed the **Robotics & AI Institute (RAI Institute)**, working on foundational robotics and AI research in cognitive AI, athletic AI, organic hardware, ethics/policy. Reinforcement learning, sim-to-real transfer, dynamic control: e.g. they use RL methods to improve robot agility, speed (e.g. improving Spot's running), and train generalizable behaviors. Public research collaboration: working with institutes, universities, partners, sharing research insights, publishing.

▪ SMART ASSISTANTS

Smart assistants will become one of the most popular ways consumers will interact with an AI. Smart assistants combine modalities to support text, images and limited agent capabilities.

COMPANY URL	DESCRIPTION
Alexa https://amazon.com	Alexa is Amazon's voice assistant service and smart-home hub. The Alexa developer site offers tools, APIs, and reference solutions for building Alexa "skills" (voice apps) and integrating with smart home devices. With the newer **Alexa+** branding, Amazon promotes a more conversational, generative-AI assistant that can perform more sophisticated tasks and maintain context.
Siri https://apple.com/siri/	**Siri** is Apple's built-in voice assistant across iOS, macOS, watchOS, HomePod, etc. It helps users make calls, send messages, control apps and devices, set reminders, query information, and more via voice commands. With **Apple Intelligence**, Siri is being enhanced to maintain conversational context, allow typed or spoken interaction, and in some cases tap into advanced services (e.g. ChatGPT) for expanded knowledge. Apple emphasizes privacy: many Siri requests are processed on-device when possible, minimizing data transmission.

COMPANY URL	DESCRIPTION
Microsoft Copilot https://copilot.microsoft.com	Microsoft positions **Copilot** as an AI companion/assistant that works across devices and apps. Within Microsoft 365, Copilot integrates into Word, Excel, Outlook, PowerPoint, Teams, etc., allowing users to draft content, analyze data, automate tasks, chat with context, and more. **Copilot Chat** is a secure AI chat assistant that can access uploaded files, generate images, and use web data; in M365 it also grounds responses in user's work data (documents, emails).
Zoom AI https://zoom.com/products/ai-assistant	Zoom's AI Companion assists in improving productivity: summarizing meetings, drafting emails/messages, synthesizing chat threads, creating tasks, etc. It integrates with meetings, chat, docs and automates tasks.
Braina https:// brainasoft.com/braina	**Braina** is a voice assistant + speech-to-text/dictation software for Windows. It supports natural language commands, dictation, and integrates with both local and cloud LLMs for advanced responses.

▪ HEALTHCARE

Healthcare applications will grow over the near future as every healthcare company will produce one. Here are a few of the popular models today.

COMPANY URL	DESCRIPTION
Suki https://www.suki.ai/	Suki provides an **AI voice assistant for clinicians**, focusing on clinical documentation. Their assistant helps clinicians by generating evidence-backed documentation from conversations, integrating into EHRs, reducing time spent charting, and improving workflow efficiency.
Corti https://www.corti.ai/	Corti specializes in AI for **medical conversations & workflows**. Their models support speech recognition tuned to medical domain, conversation understanding, and generation/transformation of clinical data. They provide tools/APIs to build voice-based healthcare workflows.
Oracle Health Clinical AI Agent https://www.oracle.com/health/clinical-suite/clinical-ai-agent/	A voice-enabled agent integrated with Oracle Health's EHR suite. It helps clinicians with **documentation, decision support, order and medication workflows**, and reduces administrative burden by surfacing contextual insights.

COMPANY URL	DESCRIPTION
Clearstep Health https://www.clearstep.health/	Clearstep offers **AI conversational agents/triage software** for patient access: symptom checkers, digital triage, patient engagement chatbot, scheduling assistance, and workflow optimization. Their agents can be embedded in websites, patient portals, SMS/IVR, etc.
Aiva Health https://www.aivahealth.com/	Aiva provides **voice/conversational assistants for nursing/hospital staff**: voice commands to control EHRs and other systems, decreasing administrative overhead for nurses, improving patient satisfaction, and enabling hands-free control of hospital systems.
Sully.ai https://www.sully.ai/	Sully.ai promotes **"AI Medical Employees"**—automated agents for tasks such as patient intake, conversational triage, multilingual interpretation, ambient/EHR scribe, and general clinical automation (documentation, scheduling).
Docus.ai https://docus.ai/	Docus positions itself as a **personal AI health assistant** for patients and doctors. For patients, it provides symptom interpretation, lab test interpretation, personalized health insights, and access to second opinions. For clinicians, it supports decision support, documentation, and analysis.

▪ SELF-DRIVING CARS

Self-driving cars and other vehicles will be a major growth area for future jobs and innovation.

COMPANY URL	DESCRIPTION
Cruise https://getcruise.com	A subsidiary of General Motors, Cruise develops autonomous vehicles for urban ride-hailing services. Their fleet includes the Cruise Origin, a fully autonomous electric vehicle designed for shared rides. Operations have been suspended following safety incidents.
Motional https://motional.com/	A joint venture between Hyundai and Aptiv, Motional focuses on deploying Level 4 autonomous vehicles for ride-hailing and delivery services. They aim to integrate driverless technology into urban mobility networks.

COMPANY URL	DESCRIPTION
Waymo https://waymo.com	An Alphabet Inc. subsidiary, Waymo operates the world's first fully autonomous ride-hailing service. Their vehicles are active in cities like Phoenix, San Francisco, and Los Angeles. Recent incidents have raised questions about traffic law enforcement for autonomous vehicles.
Spartan https://spartangrp.com	Specializes in automotive technology solutions, including inventory management and location tracking. Their focus is on providing innovative tech for dealerships rather than developing autonomous vehicles.
Tesla https://tesla.com	Known for its Full Self-Driving (FSD) package, Tesla offers advanced driver-assistance features. While not fully autonomous, Tesla's FSD aims to handle most driving tasks under human supervision.
Luminar https://luminartech.com	Provides LiDAR technology that enhances vehicle perception systems. Their technology is integrated into vehicles like the Volvo EX90 to support autonomous driving capabilities.

▪ FINANCE

Personal finance applications will help millions to better manage debt, finances and budgets during the tough economy ahead.

COMPANY URL	DESCRIPTION
AlphaSense	An AI-powered financial research platform that helps professionals in investment banking, asset management, and corporate strategy by processing vast amounts of unstructured data to surface meaningful patterns and generate actionable insights.
Betterment	A robo-advisor offering automated investing services, including portfolio selection, trading, rebalancing, and tax management, aiming to help users build wealth over the long term.
Cleo	A personal finance assistant that uses AI to provide budgeting, saving, and debt management advice through a conversational interface, targeting users in their twenties.

▪ MARKETING

Many small businesses struggle to keep up with the daily demands of effective marketing, promotion and social media. Here is a short list of companies to consider in your business or career.

COMPANY URL	DESCRIPTION
HubSpot https://www.hubspot.com	HubSpot embeds AI across CRM, marketing and sales workflows—from AI content generation and automated email subject/body recommendations to "AI agents" that can handle knowledge-base responses, route leads, and accelerate prospecting. For SMBs this means faster campaign creation, automated customer replies, and AI-driven insights that surface which leads and messages are most likely to convert, reducing manual work for small teams.
MailChimp https://mailchimp.com	Mailchimp uses AI for predicted send-times, subject-line suggestions, audience segmentation and automated content generation (copy and alt text), plus performance predictions for campaigns. SMBs get higher open/click performance and time-savings: the platform automates routine marketing tasks and helps non-specialists produce more effective email and CRM campaigns.
Canva (Magic Studio) https://canva.com	Canva's Magic Studio adds generative AI for image creation, layout generation, design suggestions and on-the-fly copywriting so small teams can produce polished social posts, display ads, and simple videos without a designer. That reduces production costs and speeds campaign rollout for SMBs while keeping assets on-brand.
Jasper https://jasper.ai	Jasper is a marketing-focused LLM platform that provides AI agents, templates and an AI studio for producing campaign copy, blog posts, ad text and personalization at scale. For SMBs it raises content velocity (more campaigns, quicker) and helps keep messaging consistent across channels without hiring dedicated writers.
Semrush https://semrush.com	Semrush combines traditional SEO data with AI-driven content tools (Content Tool Kit, AI writing assistant, and visibility tools) to generate SEO-optimized copy, content briefs and monitor how brands appear in AI search/discovery. SMBs benefit from data-backed content that's optimized for both search engines and emerging AI discovery channels.

▪ TRAVEL AND TRANSPORTATION

Many small businesses still need to travel to events, customers and operations but don't have the travel budgets of the large corporations. To keep the travel costs down and convenience high, AI can support the team. Travel can also affect logistics, routing, and other businesses.

COMPANY URL	DESCRIPTION
Navan (formerly TripActions) https://navan.com	Navan uses AI to personalize travel searches, recommend lower-cost options during booking, and automate expense capture and reconciliation. SMBs gain faster bookings that respect policy, automated expense workflows, and AI-driven savings suggestions—all useful for small finance teams managing travel.
TravelPerk https://travelperk.com	TravelPerk applies automation and intelligent policy enforcement to bookings and cancellations, plus machine-assisted rebooking and reporting. SMBs get a centralized, policy-safe travel workflow that reduces admin overhead and improves traveler experience (flexible cancellations and automated approvals).
Samsara https://samsara.com	Samsara's platform uses on-vehicle AI (dashcams, video analytics), predictive maintenance models and smart routing to detect risky events, automate driver coaching, and predict equipment failures. For SMB fleets this reduces accidents, lowers maintenance costs and improves uptime without hiring large operations teams.
OptimoRoute https://optimoroute.com	OptimoRoute applies advanced optimization algorithms and constraints-aware scheduling (time windows, skills, vehicle types) to produce efficient daily routes and driver schedules. SMB delivery and field-service businesses use it to cut driving time, reduce fuel and labor costs, and scale routing without extra dispatch staff.
Routific https://routific.com	Routific offers an AI-powered routing engine and API (leveraging many ML models) that generates practical, driver-friendly routes and ETAs; it emphasizes quick, small-fleet use and integrates proof-of-delivery and customer updates. Small delivery operations benefit from lower delivery costs, better ETAs and simpler operations.

▪ SOCIAL MEDIA

Social media presence is a must for many corporations, but the measurable ROI is hard to determine. AI solutions offer the opportunity to reduce the effort and increase the presence.

COMPANY URL	DESCRIPTION
Hootsuite (OwlyWriter/OwlyGPT) https://hootsuite.com	Hootsuite's OwlyWriter/OwlyGPT features generate captions, post ideas, hashtag suggestions and even AI images; it can summarize competitor activity and suggest tone/formulae (AIDA, PAS). SMB social teams save hours on ideation and drafting while maintaining a consistent posting cadence and optimizing reach.
Buffer https://buffer.com	Buffer's AI assistant generates post variations, repurposes content and suggests optimizations tailored to each platform; it speeds content production, enables rapid A/B copy testing, and helps small teams maintain a consistent multi-platform presence with less manual effort.
Sprout Social https://sproutsocial.com	Sprout's AI and automation access historical social data to provide AI-assisted content creation, social listening, trend insights and influencer workflow automation. SMBs gain data-driven content recommendations, quicker responses to customers, and centralized ad/content analytics.
Later https://later.com	Later includes an AI Caption Writer, hashtag suggestion tools and visual-first scheduling that can auto-generate captions from images and recommend best post times. For SMBs focused on Instagram/visual platforms, Later speeds creative workflows and helps maximize organic reach with minimal staff.
AdEspresso (by Hootsuite)/ similar ad tools https://adespresso.com	(AdEspresso) uses automation and data-driven ad-creation templates to test ad copy and creative combinations quickly; it optimizes bids and audiences based on performance signals. SMB advertisers use it to run lean, higher-performing ad tests without ad-ops expertise.

- RETAIL

Whole Foods

COMPANY URL	DESCRIPTION
Shopify (Shopify Magic & Sidekick) https://shopify.com	Shopify's Magic and Sidekick provide generative tools to build stores from prompts (AI Store Builder), auto-generate product descriptions/images, optimize email campaigns and offer an AI assistant that analyzes store data and suggests promotions/pricing. SMB retailers dramatically shorten store setup time, scale product content, and get actionable insights without hiring outside.
Lightspeed https://lightspeedhq.com	Lightspeed has rolled out AI Showroom and related AI features that generate an online storefront from POS inventory, create themed product pages, and deliver merchandising suggestions. This helps independent retailers quickly create a modern online presence and synchronize inventory without dev teams.

NOTES

1. BBC Politics: YouTube Channel, "Godfather of AI on AI Exceed human intelligence, and it 'trying to take over.'" *BBC Newsnight*, May 2024, https://www.youtube.com/watch?v=MGJpR591oaM.
2. Greg Broadhead, "Q-Star: Harnessing AI for Enhanced Logical Inference and self-supporting learning," *Medium*, January 3, 2024, https://gregbroadhead.medium.com/q-star-harnessing-ai-for-enhanced-logical-inference-and-self-supporting-learning-87ed05b6562d.
3. *SingularityNET*, https://singularitynet.io/.
4. Eka Roivainen, "I Gave ChatGPT an IQ Test. Here's What I Discovered," *Scientific American*, March 8, 2023, https://www.scientificamerican.com/article/i-gave-chatgpt-an-iq-test-heres-what-i-discovered/.
5. Martin Mezka "Why AI will get 10X Better," *Medium*, November 25, 2024, https://medium.com/@martinmezka/why-ai-will-get-10x-better-a-look-at-the-accelerating-future-of-artificial-intelligence-bcd44757057c.
6. Hartman Neven, "Google Quantum AI Selected for DARPA QBI," *Google Quantum Blog*, September 9, 2025, https://blog.google/innovation-and-ai/technology/research/google-quantum-ai-selected-darpa-qbi/.
7. Hiawatha Bray, "MIT Scientists, tech leaders call for Six Month Pause in artificial intelligence deployment," *Boston Globe*, March 30, 2023, https://www.bostonglobe.com/2023/03/29/business/mit-scientists-tech-leaders-call-pause-artificial-intelligence-research/.
8. *World Economic Forum*, https://www.weforum.org/.
9. Daniel I. Weiner, "Citizen United Explained," *Brennen Center for Justice*, January 29, 2025, https://www.brennancenter.org/our-work/research-reports/citizens-united-explained.
10. ALM Corp, "AI Job Displacement Statistics 2026-2030," *ALM Corp*, March 13, 2026, https://almcorp.com/blog/ai-job-displacement-statistics/.
11. David Edwards, "McKinsey warns AI and robots could automate 40 percent of US jobs by 2030," *Robotics & Automation News*, November 26, 2025, https://roboticsandautomationnews.com/2025/11/26/mckinsey-warns-ai-and-robots-could-automate-40-percent-of-us-jobs-by-2030/97003/.
12. Jake Angelo, "Anthropic just mapped out which jobs AI could potentially replace. A 'Great Recession for white-collar workers' is absolutely possible," *Fortune*, March 6, 2026, https://fortune.com/2026/03/06/ai-job-losses-report-anthropic-research-great-recession-for-white-collar-workers/.
13. World Economic Forum, "WEF Future of Jobs Report 2025," *World Economic Forum*, January 2025, https://reports.weforum.org/docs/WEF_Future_of_Jobs_Report_2025.pdf.

14. CLICKVISION, "AI Job Displacement Statistics," *CLICKVISION*, February 4, 2026, https://click-vision.com/ai-job-displacement-statistics.
15. Future Investment Initiative Institute, "AI and the Future Impact Report 2024," *FII Institute*, January 24, 2024, https://fii-institute.org/publication/ai-impact-report-2024/.
16. American Immigration Council, "Senate Approves Unprecedented Spending for Mass Deportation," *American Immigration Council*, July 1, 2025, https://www.americanimmigrationcouncil.org/press-release/congress-approves-unprecedented-funding-mass-detention-deportation-2025/.
17. *World Economic Forum*, https://www.weforum.org/.
18. *Rehan School*, https://rehanschool.com/.
19. World Health Organization, "Climate Inaction is Claiming Millions of Lives," *World Health Organization*, October 29, 2025, https://www.who.int/news/item/29-10-2025-climate-inaction-is-claiming-millions-of-lives-every-year--warns-new-lancet-countdown-report.
20. National Institute of Standards and Technology, "AI Standards," *NIST*, May 5, 2026 https://www.nist.gov/artificial-intelligence/ai-standards.
21. Ibid.
22. Ibid.
23. Ibid.
24. Ibid.
25. Ibid.
26. Dan Robitzski, "MSN Fires Journalist and Replaces with AI," *Futurism*, June 1, 2020, https://futurism.com/the-byte/msn-fires-journalists-replaces-ai.

ABOUT THE AUTHOR

GUY MORRIS is a retired Fortune 500 executive with a four-decade career spanning software, high-tech, and global energy, including leadership roles with IBM, Burroughs, Occidental Petroleum, Oracle, and Microsoft. Known as an innovator and strategic thinker, he has led initiatives in finance, business strategy, enterprise quality, PMO, consulting, sales, and new market development—translating emerging technology into real-world business impact.

With academic training in economics and finance and a minor in computer science, Guy earned a full-scholarship MBA at the University of Arizona. Early in his career, he gained international recognition for developing a macroeconomic model that outperformed Federal Reserve forecasts and influenced modern economic modeling approaches. The model relied on early algorithmic pattern-recognition techniques that anticipated the principles behind today's artificial intelligence systems, placing him at the intersection of economics and machine intelligence long before AI became mainstream.

Throughout his career, Guy helped global enterprises evaluate, implement, and scale breakthrough technologies to create competitive advantage and transform operations. His work with emerging systems often paralleled key milestones in the evolution of machine intelligence.

Beyond the corporate world, Guy's life has been unusually diverse: a published songwriter with Disney Records, Coast Guard charter captain, diver, adventurer, entrepreneur, inventor, and award-winning thriller author. His experiences range from cartel death threats in Latin America to shark diving in Moorea, from boardroom negotiations to recording studios, and from childhood homelessness to global business leadership. He brings this breadth of experience to his writing, combining realism, technical insight, and human drama to explore the profound challenges and opportunities facing humanity in the age of artificial intelligence.

www.ingramcontent.com/pod-product-compliance
Lightning Source LLC
La Vergne TN
LVHW040515210926
848480LV00005BA/1463